✧ Y0-ARM-168

This is a book for parents . . .

Specifically, it is for parents who share a painful bond for it looks at the problems of youth rebellion. Lest the reader be betrayed, however, it should be understood that this is not a book on how to prevent rebellion. Nor does it offer an abundance of advice on dealing with rebellion in the home.

It is a book written from the perspective of the parent who has tried everything but who is, nonetheless, faced with a casualty. It attempts to answer only one question. After the parent has done everything possible for his child, what can the parent do for himself?

Is There Life After Johnny?

JOY P. GAGE

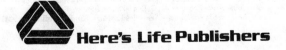
Here's Life Publishers

First printing, August 1989

Published by
HERE'S LIFE PUBLISHERS, INC.
P. O. Box 1576
San Bernardino, CA 92402

© 1989, Joy P. Gage
All rights reserved.
Printed in the United States of America.

Library of Congress Cataloging-in-Publication Data
Gage, Joy P.
     Is there life after Johnny? : standing strong through your
child's rebellion / Joy P. Gage.
       p.   cm.
     ISBN 0-89840-255-7
     1. Parent and child.   2. Youth — Family relationships.
3. Problem children.   I. Title.
HQ755.85.G33   1989
306.874 — dc 20   89-34832
                      CIP

Unless otherwise indicated, Scripture quotations are from *The King James
Version* of the Bible. Scripture quotations designated TLB are from *The
Living Bible,* © 1971 by Tyndale House Publishers, Wheaton, Illinois. Scrip-
ture quotations designated NIV are from *The Holy Bible, New International
Version,* © 1973, 1978, 1984 by the International Bible Society, published by
the Zondervan Bible Publishers, Grand Rapids, Michigan.

For More Information, Write:

L.I.F.E. — P.O. Box A399, Sydney South 2000, Australia
Campus Crusade for Christ of Canada — Box 300, Vancouver, B.C., V6C 2X3, Canada
Campus Crusade for Christ — Pearl Assurance House, 4 Temple Row, Birmingham, B2 5HG, England
Lay Institute for Evangelism — P.O. Box 8786, Auckland 3, New Zealand
Campus Crusade for Christ — P.O. Box 240, Colombo Court Post Office, Singapore 9117
Great Commission Movement of Nigeria — P.O. Box 500, Jos, Plateau State Nigeria, West Africa
Campus Crusade for Christ International — Arrowhead Springs, San Bernardino, CA 92414, U.S.A.

for him
with whom I cried
and for our three
who also brought us laughter

CONTENTS

PART FOUR
The Parents Face a Casualty

PART FIVE
The Parents' Right to Life

PART SIX
The Parents' Gift of Love

PART ONE

The Plight
of the Parent

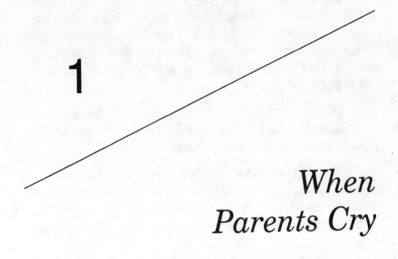

When Parents Cry

"Where did we go wrong?" "What can we do?" "Why did it happen to *us?*" "Why? Why? Why?"

Such are the cries of parents everywhere who face the problems of estranged sons and daughters. It is a rare home which has not lost an offspring to the drug culture, the sexual revolution, the occult or some pseudo-religious group. Likewise, it is a rare parent whose initial reaction, when confronted with the problem, is not guilt and self-condemnation.

So much has been written about youth in rebellion. Volumes have been produced in an attempt to analyze, defend, explain or correct the younger generation, but not enough has been said to encourage, help or comfort the parents in their heartache, disappointment and confusion.

Many have examined teens to determine how their rebellion will affect the future of society in general.

Few have thought it necessary to speculate on how those actions affect the parent. While conjecturing on the outcome of the collective younger generation's actions, we have not yet seen the full effects on a generation of parents who are debilitated by disillusionment, defeat and depression.

Although the plight of the parent has been largely ignored, the fact remains: When Johnny rebels, the parents—indeed, the whole family—suffer.

With little regard for benumbed and bewildered parents, the unstructured generation has marched off in quest of something essentially its own, and in the process entire families have lost something which was corporately theirs.

Survey results

Johnny rebels because he wants the right to live his own life, yet in so doing, he disrupts the lives of all the others in the family. What he sees as a justifiable bid for his chosen lifestyle may constitute an irreversible blow to the family lifestyle. In altering his own future, Johnny may also permanently alter that of his parents and of his siblings. For them, time becomes a commodity measured by Johnny's actions. His act of rebellion becomes the dividing point between all their yesterdays and all their tomorrows. In their worst moments they pray that the latter will be mercifully few.

Through it all, Johnny remains oblivious to the fact that in seizing his right to live he has thrust his family into an emotional limbo. His is a generation of free spirits. They have been both praised as the most promising generation and condemned as the ugly generation. However the young people are perceived, their parents are troubled just the same. In a very real sense these parents have become the disillusioned generation.

Syndicated columnist Ann Landers once polled her readers as to whether or not they would choose to be parents if they had it to do over. Out of 10,000 respondents, the answer was a resounding "no" from 7,000. Having balanced all the negative against all the positive, these parents had concluded that the heartaches outweighed the joys. They considered the experience of parenthood altogether too traumatic to merit ever going through again.

Why it's so serious

When the nation's parents so adamantly voice their defeat and disillusionment, surely it is time society listened. Surely it is a serious matter.

Specifically, I believe it is serious for three reasons. **First**, it is serious because it affects so many homes. For every parent who wrote in, how many were there who could not admit how they really felt?

Second, it is serious because of the variety of homes affected. As a committed Christian parent, I have been keenly aware of the number of my peers who are disillusioned over the rebellion of a son or a daughter. I also have seen parents from other backgrounds who are crushed because a son or a daughter has opted for a life-style contrary to their own. Whether a conservative parent, a liberal parent, a Christian parent, or a parent who has little time for spiritual things, with whatever philosophy one approaches parenthood, the parent hopes his offspring will be a permanent part of his family life. When the child rebels and becomes estranged, he leaves behind him parents who are, at the very least, bewildered, and at the worst, shattered.

Third, disillusionment is serious because it is so

emotionally debilitating to the average parent. In zombie fashion the parent moves through the daily routine. Whatever he does in the way of work is done through automatic reactions or not at all. The mental process is reduced to one thought: *I can't believe it. It's not happening. It can't be real.*

One mother helplessly watched her daughter rush into a bizarre marriage. Then she had to cope with the emotional effect of the marriage upon her daughter as well as the practical aspects of the divorce. She expresses it thus: "Sometimes, when I am thinking about my daughter or taking care of our grandchild, I feel overwhelmed by disorientation, a feeling similar to the loss of physical balance from an inner ear infection. It comes entirely as a surprise, and I can scarcely believe that our daughter actually did what she did, or that her baby is really real."

Sooner or later, depending on the personality and the circumstances, the parent will awaken from this state of disbelief and face the truth. *It is real. It has happened. My world has fallen apart. It has come down around my ears and I haven't the vaguest idea how to put it back together again.*

"It's so easy to slip into bitterness after the shock or grief has worn off," writes one mother. But bitterness is not conducive to putting one's world in place again. The parent must begin to rebuild his life before bitterness makes a permanent inroad.

Rebuilding a workable relationship

Rebuilding your life will not be accomplished overnight, and even when it is done your world will not be the same as before—but it must be done. Putting your world together again does not mean solving Johnny's problem or restoring the old relationship between Johnny and the family. It means solving the problems Johnny created for the family in the best way you can. It means finding a different relationship with Johnny. It means building a new family life for those who remain. It means making family plans which will not be contingent on Johnny's reactions or actions. It means picking up the pieces and getting on with the business of living.

In time, it will mean welcoming Johnny back into your world if he can respect it as your world. From the beginning, rebuilding your world must involve finding a workable relationship with Johnny. When the estranged offspring is of age, the workable relationship will never be found unless the parents accept Johnny's right to make his own mistakes.

The last-ditch stand

This is a fact which many parents find hard to deal with. Before they can face it honestly there is apt to be a final hysterical scene in which the parents beg the child to reconsider his actions. The parent experiences an "I've got to do something" feeling which borders on panic. The resulting confrontation can be ugly. There may be further attempts to engage friends or relatives, the minister or the doctor to abort the action.

There is very little a last-ditch stand can accomplish, though, except to hasten the realization of the brutal truth. There is nothing you can do. At that moment it is terribly frustrating to realize that your government can send a man to the moon and back but no one can tell you how to stop your child from destroying himself.

Forewarning

For the parent who has had some forewarning, the feeling of frustration may be magnified. Through a series of events, he realizes that his teen has set out on a course which is not only contrary to all the parent's values but is also clearly self-destructive for the child. Yet, for one reason or another, the parent is powerless to change Johnny's direction. No amount of counseling, coercing, or hysterics can stop the inevitable.

The parent tries: "You should stay in school." "You should not be dating that girl." "Stay away from drugs."

But it is no use. It must be rather like watching your child be consumed by a terminal illness.

Sylvia Vogel, a Jewish mother, tells her story concerning her daughter's decision to join a cult. The story reveals that, from the beginning, the mother was aware of the implications of her daughter's actions. Yet she was unable to stop them. On Mother's Day, Sylvia Vogel received word that the cult leaders had picked her Jewish daughter and a black seminary student she hardly knew as one of 705 "perfect matches" for marriage.

According to Mrs. Vogel, her daughter was "emotionally bankrupt" when she joined the cult. "She started having severe emotional problems when she was thirteen years old. Her father had a massive coronary and was seriously ill for four years until he died. She became a loner."

Ellen Vogel made her first contact with the cult during the time her father was ill. She went to one of their meetings. Afterwards, Mrs. Vogel said, "She came home and said, 'They're all wonderful. They're young and happy and so beautiful.'

"I said, 'What about your religion? ' "

Ellen was raised a conservative Jew with ten years of Hebrew schooling. She could read, write and speak Hebrew, and she has studied French, Russian, Japanese and Korean.

"Her brother is a rabbi," said her mother. "This is a girl who knew all the prayers. She didn't even have to open a book."

Two days after her father died in September 1973, Ellen moved out, telling her mother she was leaving to work with the cult.

"When she left she told me, 'I'm Jewish and I'll always be Jewish,' " her mother said. But since then her mother said she has had little to do with the Jewish religion.

About all she can do for the present is "hope and pray" Mrs. Vogel said, adding there isn't a night she goes to bed that she doesn't "think about my baby."[1]

No warning

Mrs. Vogel was one of those parents who had some warning but could not stop the chain of events. For many parents there is no such warning. Suddenly one day, when everything seems to be going just right, the word comes. A telephone call from college: "I'm dropping out to join a commune." A discreet message from a friend: "Your son is living with his girlfriend." A surprise visit to your married daughter: She is sharing her bed with one man, her couch with another, and her husband is overseas. A tearful call from your daughter-in-law: Your twenty-one-year-old son has abandoned her for another woman. The juvenile authorities come: Your sixteen-year-old has been picked up on drug charges.

Whatever the problem, however the parent learns of it, the discovery has to be among the greatest traumas of parenthood. It is as though a terrible accident has wrenched your child away from you. In that moment you know that life can never again be quite the same.

Looking for causes

One of the faults of human nature is that we are forever approaching our problems by analyzing them and establishing cause and effect. We get all involved in theories and statistics and forget about flesh-and-blood realities.

"Who caused the mass youth rebellion?" we ask. And the theories pour in. The parents were too strict. No, they were too lenient. They overindulged their children. Not true—they neglected them. The parents gave them everything but their time. The children had no spiritual guidance. Or to the contrary—religion had been crammed down their throats.

From all the theories come a fresh set of statistics. The trouble is that, even if it were possible to analyze the cause correctly, deciding who was responsible for it does not diminish the pain inflicted by it. Meticulous charts of theories and statistics are of little comfort to a parent whose offspring has suddenly become a statistic.

Dealing with effects

I believe it is time to look beyond the cause and deal with the effects. So this is not a book about what caused Johnny's rebellion or how it could have been prevented. Nor is it a book to tell you how to handle Johnny in the crisis of the rebellion. It is a practical book for parents who are trying to find their way out of the depression and disillusionment brought about by Johnny's rebellion.

Three major areas will be considered: (1) uncovering the causes of disillusionment (this involves parental problems with standards); (2) coping with the casualty; and (3) discovering life "after Johnny."

I am not sure if there is a foolproof formula to prevent rebellion. Neither do I attempt here to tell you how to correct the rebellion. However, if you are a parent faced with this problem, I hope to encourage you to put the past with its devastating disappointments behind you. If you know someone who faces this problem, I encourage you to show compassion. When parents hurt, it is a serious matter. It is urgent that they know someone cares.

Too often when parents cry, they cry alone. Some cry quietly. Some cry hysterically. Some cry only behind closed doors. They cry for all their yesterdays. They cry because suddenly there are no tomorrows. They cry for what might have been. They cry for what surely is to be. They cry out of anger. They cry out of frustration. They cry because they are afraid God does not hear them. And I think, most of all, they cry because they are desperately afraid that when parents cry, no one listens.

PART TWO

Setting
Standards
for the
Wrong Reasons

2

The Care and Feeding of Disillusionment

Many writers who address the problem of youth in rebellion give considerable space to the question, "How do kids get that way?" Since I am more concerned about dealing with the effects of rebellion than theorizing its causes, I would rather consider the question, "How do parents get that way?"

Why do parents react as they do to the problem of rebellion? How is it that parents can survive some of life's most devastating experiences and then be completely disillusioned by the actions of a son or daughter?

Parents predispose themselves to disillusionment

Disillusionment is sometimes born in the simple act of doing all the right things for all the wrong reasons. Parental disillusionment often stems from setting the right standards for the wrong reasons. It is one thing to set guidelines because one believes them to be right. It is quite another to set guidelines because one believes them to be the key to absolute prevention of rebellion.

The parent who fails to make this distinction sets himself up for disappointment. Assuming total responsibility for the outcome of parental training is unrealistic. Parents who set unrealistic goals concerning parental training are prime targets for disillusionment.

Case history: My disillusionment and how I acquired it

To say I was disappointed the first time one of our daughters did something contrary to our values is putting it mildly. She was legally an adult and was on her own, but that did not lessen my feelings of responsibility. My life fell apart. Coping was impossible until I accepted the fact that I could not change what she was doing. Once I did that, it no longer made sense to ask, "Why is she doing this?" Admitting that I had no control over her actions, I began to concentrate on my own reactions.

I asked myself, "Why am I so devastated by what she is doing?" Only by frankly facing the past did I find the answers I sought. It didn't happen overnight, but eventually I discovered that through my unrealistic attitude toward parental training I had set myself up for disappointment. That discovery was the beginning of my emotional healing. As a reader, you cannot benefit from my solution unless you understand some of what contributed to my problem.

I never expected the life of a parent to be trouble free. I knew that along with the joys would come assorted heartaches. I expected to do some crying. I understood that in giving life to a tiny human being my husband and I would make ourselves vulnerable to a certain amount of pain. However, for the most part, I anticipated parenthood as a wonderful experience. As we looked forward to the birth of our first child, time stood still. Yet my joy mingled with sober reflections. For me, conception was singularly different from all of life's previous experiences. There was a pleasant finality about it which caused me to look at life a bit more seriously.

I believe that I was quite realistic about the negative aspects of childbearing. I recognized that, although the percentage is small, miscarriages, stillbirths and birth defects are all risks which accompany conception.

The instant my firstborn arrived I asked the doctor, "How soon will you test her to see if she is completely normal?" Of course it already was obvious that she looked normal, but I wanted to make sure that she could see and hear. I never took the miracle of birth for granted. I gave thanks to God that our firstborn was normal. And our second. And our third.

Our little boy

My fourth pregnancy was abnormal from the beginning. So much so that only I knew I was pregnant. The doctor remained unconvinced. He scheduled my appointments at two-week intervals until we could agree on the diagnosis. When he finally came to a decision, I was not prepared for what went with it.

"You're pregnant," he said, "but you have only about a ten percent chance of carrying it. The fetus is not developing normally."

"Suppose I do carry it?" I blurted out. "Will the baby be abnormal?"

His answer was evasive. "I don't think you will carry it," was all he would say.

In a rather confused state of mind I walked the few short blocks home. All I could think of was, *What if*

*I do carry this baby? And what if it's a boy? And what if
he's abnormal?* For some reason the thought of having
an abnormal boy after three normal girls seemed the
worst possible outcome of my condition.

As it turned out, the fetus (a boy) was normal, but
a fibroid tumor complicated my pregnancy. That, plus a
severe case of the mumps, precipitated a miscarriage and
ended my childbearing years.

Because I was aware of the implications from the
beginning, experiencing the miscarriage was not as traumatic for me as it is for many other women. In the years
to follow, I did have some fleeting moments when I
longed for that incompletely formed little boy who left
us before I ever held him in my arms. For the most part,
though, I recognized that our loss was simply one of those
risks which accompany conception. I counted my blessings that out of four pregnancies we had gained three
normal, healthy girls.

Noble ambitions

Somehow I was not so well prepared to face some
of the other risks which accompany parenthood. I totally conditioned myself to believe that if I trained my
children properly, the result would be young adult offspring who would have the desire and the wisdom to
make all the right choices. There would be no risk involved. I was sure that if I did everything exactly right,
my adult children would never disappoint me by doing
what they knew to be wrong.

Numerous formulas proffered by well-meaning
experts feed this common misconception. These experts
infer that if you follow directions, your child will never
rebel and his life will never fall apart. In effect, they offer
money-back guarantees. Certainly no one ever tells you,

"There will be some casualties along the way."

The formulas for successful parenting vary from the highly permissive to the very strict. No matter what approach one takes toward parenthood, the average parent chooses that approach because he believes he can control the results.

The liberal parent sets out to eliminate the strict code of conduct so Johnny will have no reason to rebel. When Johnny finds a reason anyway, the parent is bewildered. The committed Christian parent teaches a strict code of conduct and tries to counter the influence of the world upon Johnny. When Johnny opts for a loose lifestyle with everything the world has to offer, the parent is crushed.

Their approaches are different, but these parents share one thing in common. Their reason for raising Johnny by a certain standard is to insure that Johnny continues to live by that standard. The results are supposed to be predictable—but they aren't.

The truth is, the parents' only responsibility is to train the child. However wisely or conscientiously, however unselfishly the parents accept this responsibility, they must always remember there is no guarantee that Johnny will not rebel. Parents who assume differently set themselves up for needless heartache.

My sense of personal failure and frustration over my daughter's problem was overwhelming. The feeling was intensified because I had accepted my responsibilities as a mother so conscientiously. They included reading all the books, avoiding mistakes I observed in others, and praying daily for my children.

My husband being a minister put me in a unique position to observe parents from all walks of life. Our churches had parents whose children were a joy, but there were also parents whose hearts were broken by their children. Even as my heart ached for them, I determined not to allow this to happen to me.

When our children were still very small we had a grandmotherly friend living nearby who was fond of quoting the adage, "When children are little they walk on your feet. When they are big, they walk on your heart." I was not quite thirty and I had more answers than when I became forty-five. I saw little need for a toddler to walk on a mother's feet, and I was certain that it was completely unnecessary for a grown child to walk on a mother's heart.

Although it sounds ridiculous to me now, at that time I was convinced I could make that old saying work in reverse. By teaching my children to respect my feet, I thought that I could assure myself they would always respect my heart. Since my biggest aim in life was to be a good wife and a good mother, I assumed my children would respond to my noble ambitions and would never do anything which would cause me undue pain or humiliation.

I know now that, while children are the source of life's brightest moments, the parent-child relationship will also inflict a certain amount of pain. It cannot be avoided. It comes with the territory. Still, as a mother of toddlers, I was idealistic. I went through each day with my blinders intact, involving myself in the all-important task of teaching my children not to walk on my feet.

A daring magazine article

I recall reading a magazine article at that stage of my life which left me very unsettled because I recognized in it a warning aimed directly at me. The article pointed out that it was sheer folly to allow the key to one's own happiness to be tied in to the responses of another person.

I accepted without question that the writer of that article had people like me in mind. Certainly the thing which would give me the greatest happiness would be to see our children respond properly to their parental training. I was not just training them because it was my responsibility; I was training them because their response to that training was essential to my happiness. Had anyone suggested their response might disappoint me, I would have said, "Then I'll try harder. I'll find a way." After all, there had never been a lack of magazine articles to help me find a better way.

This was the first article I had seen which implied that parental happiness should never be sought through a foolproof formula for successful child-rearing. Many people wrote about how parents could succeed at their job. Only one impertinent writer dared to suggest that it is a foolish parent who depends on the outcome of his child-rearing efforts to bring personal happiness. Only this writer hinted, in some indefinable way, that there was absolutely no relationship between protecting one's feet and protecting one's heart.

The road to disillusionment

The article uncovered my blind spot, and in its place I built a defense. I knew that, as Christian parents, we had resources which the writer had not taken into consideration. My husband and I depended on the Lord for strength and on His Word for wisdom to raise our children properly. Surely the Lord would control the result of that training. Nothing could have convinced me I was heading blindly down the road to disappointment.

A dear friend of many years tells how she traveled a similar road. "It took me a long time to see that I had set myself up for heartache and disappointment," she confessed. "My children would all grow up to 'serve the Lord' as ministers or missionaries, or through some kind of career service in related ministries. Hadn't we dedicated each one to the Lord privately and publicly? Didn't we have daily devotions, teach them to pray, encourage them to study their Bibles, take them to services, send them to camp, teach them right from wrong and keep them away from 'the world'?" When faced with the problem of a rebellious teen, she felt the confusion and disillusionment common to all such parents.

The story could be repeated over and over again. Many conscientious Christian parents experience heartache because that sweet little child who once recited Bible verses on Daddy's knee is now enmeshed in the drug scene, caught up with some cult, or sharing an apartment with a member of the opposite sex.

Who's responsible?

These disillusioned parents spend half their time asking, "Have I failed God?" and the other half asking, "Has God failed me?" At no time does it occur to them to ask, "Is it Johnny who has failed?"

On the one hand the parent reasons, *If I am responsible for Johnny's training, I must have failed God.* On the other hand he reasons, *If God is supposed to be controlling the results, why didn't He prevent Johnny's rebellion?* In the confusion who ever thinks to ask, "What is Johnny's responsibility here?"

Like my friends, when I faced the casualty I found myself in a maze of confusion, with no escape. After about six weeks of this, I was beginning to wish I had never left my mother's womb. Then one day when I least expected it, I received some startling advice on the subject of parental responsibility.

During an informal after-dinner conversation, a visiting minister told those parents present that parents must expect some casualties along the way. After so many experts had tantalized us with formulas for success, this man was telling us there would be casualties along the way? So many had said, "You were too strict"; or "You were too lenient." Now this one said, "No matter how you try, there are going to be some casualties."

No success formula

Another mother who happened to be present that day sparked our entire conversation with her questions. Her children were rapidly approaching their teenage years. With the same speed, she was approaching the panic years. All around her, she viewed teenagers from Christian homes making bad decisions, rejecting their training, turning away from God. Deacons, pastors, Sunday school teachers—hardly a home had been untouched by the problem of a rebellious young person. With increasing concern, this mother was searching for that one key which everyone else had missed. If only someone could tell her how to raise her children in such a way that they would make all the right decisions! In essence, she was searching for that formula which, if followed to the letter, would guarantee success.

Instead she was told there are no such formulas. Success is not guaranteed. Results are sometimes disappointing. "We must train our children because that is our responsibility," the visiting minister emphasized. "Just remember, as parents we are only accountable for how we train our children. They must account for what they do with that training."

Listening to his words, I felt an unnecessary and extremely heavy weight of responsibility begin to slip away. My standards for child-rearing did not change. I didn't mentally revise my methods—only my motives. The disillusionment which had engulfed me did not instantly disappear, but that day there was a beginning. There was a light at the end of the very dark tunnel. I made a firm first step toward emotional recovery as I came to terms with the question of responsibility. Mine. My daughter's. God's. There would be more tears, and other problems with other daughters, but I would not again set myself up for disappointment through confused thinking over responsibility.

Not all parents have problems with a misplaced sense of responsibility, but all parents who seek recovery from disillusionment must begin with the same step. They must deal with the past.

Looking back is inevitable. It can only be valuable if it is done from the right perspective. So long as there are Johnnys who go astray there will be parents who ask, "Am I to blame?" and, "Why is Johnny acting this way?"

I looked at our past and asked all those questions. All I found was an overwhelming sense of failure, the common bond of all parents who cry. Then I dealt with the past by asking, "Did I set myself up for disappointment?" and, "Why am I reacting this way?" Only then did I discover the underlying causes of my own disillusionment. Only then did emotional recovery begin.

3

Train a Child or Control a Life?

This chapter may not be for you. Not every parent sets himself or herself up for disappointment through faulty theology, but after I had begun work on this book something happened which convinced me of the need to include this chapter.

I read an article which stated that when young adult offspring of Christian parents rebel, it is the fault of the parent. The author based his reasoning on Proverbs 22:6: "Train up a child in the way he should go: and when he is old, he will not depart from it." Some Christian parents and religious authority figures look upon that verse as a guarantee that a child, properly trained, will never rebel at any age.

The writer of the article concluded that the verse constitutes a promise to the parent. He further concluded that since God does not fail to keep His promises, it must follow that rebellion against childhood training can result only from parental failure. I realized then that no book of this nature would be complete unless it gives the parent some answers for this rather cruel indictment.

That very day I sat down and read the Book of Proverbs through in one sitting. I underlined in red every verse which spoke directly of the responsibility of the youth. I underlined in blue every verse which spoke directly of the responsibility of the parent. By conservative estimate there are four times more verses which deal with the responsibility of the youth.

Taken in the context of the entire book of Proverbs, 22:6 can hardly be interpreted as placing the total responsibility for adolescent rebellion upon the parent. The admonition to the parent is to train the child. The promise is that when he is old he will not depart from that training. The word doesn't mean mature and it doesn't mean older. It means old. The problems of rebellion concern a third age bracket, the youth.

Are your problems compounded by friends, peers, or religious authority figures who use Proverbs 22:6 to tell you, "It has to be your fault"? Are you disillusioned because you have realized, "I can train my child but I cannot control his life from the cradle to the grave"? If so, this chapter is especially for you. Let's consider what the rest of Proverbs has to say.

The proverbs which deal with parental training and rebellious youth fall loosely into five categories: (1) specific responsibility of the parent-teacher; (2) specific responsibility of the youth-learner; (3) the accountability of the youth; (4) the unmerited suffering of the parents of a rebel; and (5) some specific ways in which to deal with a rebel.

1. **Responsibility of the parent-teacher**

Discipline: The child needs it

The parent is charged with the responsibility of disciplining the child. Several reasons are cited. First, the child needs discipline. If you fail to discipline a child in his early life, you will ruin him (19:18, see TLB). "A youngster's heart is filled with rebellion, but punishment will drive it out of him" (22:15, TLB).

Certainly we all have seen undisciplined young children. They are out of control because parents will not put forth the time and effort required to discipline them. These children have problems which are a direct result of parental failure. On the other hand, there are many well-disciplined children who grow up to rebel against parental values. Later chapters will bear this out. The parent should discipline the child because that is his responsibility. He is charged with controlling a *child,* not controlling an entire life.

Discipline: It proves the parent's love

The parent must also discipline his child to show his love for the child. In fact, "If you refuse to discipline your son, it proves you don't love him" (13:24, TLB). I have seen the truth of this principle attested to by youth who were going through a time of rebellion. One young woman told her family she wanted to live her own life in her own way without their interference. After several years she was still living her own life, but she had completely reversed herself on the interference issue. She felt that a negative response from her family was better than none at all and told them so. She had found that, when her parents withdrew their guidance (she was of legal age), their lack of input made her unsure of their love. Their discipline while she was growing up was recognized as an indication of their love.

The responsibility of the parent-teacher may include physical punishment. Sometimes mere words are not enough. "Scolding and spanking a child helps him to learn" (29:15, TLB).

Carl was the principal of a small rural school when we met him. He stayed in that school for sixteen years because he wanted his children to go to a school where they would receive discipline which would underscore the discipline they received at home. In discussing the problems of discipline, Carl related to us an incident which took place while he was attending summer school at a large western university.

The guest lecturer for the summer English course was a well-known writer. This lecturer stated that good teachers never need to use discipline. If the teacher makes the class interesting, the discipline will take care of itself. Carl challenged this statement. (Carl had been teaching all those years while the guest lecturer was turning out bestsellers.) The lecturer promptly invited Carl to see for himself.

"I teach a class every morning," he said. "The students are children of professors at this university. Why don't you sit in on it?"

Carl went the next day. He found a seat in the back of the room from which he could observe the teacher and the pupils. The lecturer was halfway through a very interesting period when two boys in the back of the room began to scuffle. The lecturer tried to ignore them. Then he tried to reason with them. Things got worse instead of better. The exasperated lecturer finally marched to the back of the room and physically restrained the boys. End of scuffle. End of demonstration. Carl left the room.

Sometimes mere words are just not enough!

Discipline: It drives evil from the child's heart

The parent is admonished to use punishment that hurts because it drives evil from the heart and keeps the child out of hell (23:13,14). This passage also declares that parents should not fail to correct children because discipline won't hurt, and they won't die if you use a stick on them. Certainly we cannot construe these passages to condone cruel physical punishment which does hurt too much and from which too many children do die. Obviously these children are the victims of abusive parents and we cannot use the Scriptures to rationalize such actions.

A parent who cannot control his anger while disciplining a child should never use physical punishment, but a normal and rational approach to discipline sometimes calls for a bit of pain inflicted to the child's well-padded seat of learning.

2. Responsibility of the youth-learner

The bulk of Proverbs is directed to the youth, and it places directly on them an enormous amount of responsibility for their behavior.

Seek wisdom

The initial subject of the book is the value of wisdom, and the admonition concerning gaining wisdom is directed primarily to young men. "The first step [in becoming wise] is to trust and reverence the LORD!" (1:7). The theme is later repeated as we see that "reverence and fear of God are basic to all wisdom [and that] knowing God results in every other kind of understanding" (9:10, TLB). It is significant that the key to obtaining this wisdom is not found in parental training. Rather, it is found in the individual's desire for wisdom (2:1-5).

We must assume then that while a parent can discipline a child, he cannot make him wise. Only the Lord can give wisdom. Essentially, King Solomon says that wisdom begins with reverence and trust in the Lord, plus a desire of the heart to be wise. God responds to that desire by giving wisdom.

The fact that wisdom is essential to well-being is spelled out in 1:20-30. Those who spurn wisdom are given a special warning:

> Some day when you need wisdom because you are in trouble, it will be too late. There will be no help for your anguish and distress because you chose to ignore all the facts; you refused to reverence and trust the Lord and you lack the wisdom you need (TLB paraphrased).

This person must suffer the consequences of having his own way.

The most significant fact about this initial discourse is that the responsibility is clearly and specifically placed on the learner. Only fools refuse to be taught (1:7), and sons are admonished to listen to their parents (1:8). We must assume that, however good the training, there will be some who stubbornly refuse to listen. Those who do listen will learn and will gain many honors.

Proverbs 23:22 repeats this theme as young men are admonished to listen to their father's advice and to despise not an old mother's experience. I like to think that this even gives me scriptural license to say, "Now when I was your age . . ."

Assume responsibility

Not only are the young admonished to listen to their parents, but they also are told to assume responsibility for important areas of their own lives. They are to take care to stay away from bad company, to refuse to emulate the actions of the wicked, and to guard their affections. In fact, they are to choose to follow the advice of their parents instead of the suggestions of the wrong kind of friends (1:1-15). The youths are to assume responsibility for turning their backs on young toughs who rob, steal and kill. They are to stay away from people with whom crime has become a way of life.

What does this really say to us about the responsibility of the parent and the responsibility of the youth? Certainly as parents we are to teach our children all of these principles, but we note that the principles are not given to parents as a training pattern. These principles are given to youth as a living pattern. It is the young people to whom these proverbs are addressed.

There is a practical reason youth must assume responsibility for their actions. Unlike young children, youth are often away from home without parental supervision. Once a child is old enough to attend school, community or church functions without parental chaperoning, the parent cannot be 100 percent sure what the child is doing every minute. The parents admonish their young people to make the right choices they have been taught to make.

Avoid the ways of the wicked

Proverbs, chapter 4, deals at length with avoiding the ways of the wicked. The youth are told to avoid the haunts of the wicked—to find their company elsewhere. An evangelist friend who is a former heroin addict relates how his entire life of crime began when he, as a young boy, began frequenting one of the city's biggest hangouts for gamblers and addicts. He knew it was wrong but he did it anyway. Today one of his chief messages to young people is that a man is known by the company he keeps (Proverbs 13:20)—and that he is also greatly influenced by that company. The biblical principle to avoid wicked company is a solid principle.

Guard affections

Guarding one's affections is important because the affections "influence everything else in your life" (4:23, TLB). While we as parents must teach our children this principle, we also have to face the fact that our sons and daughters may make some wrong choices in this area. Affections can be controlled, but they can be controlled only by the individual. As parents we can train and we can pray, but that son or daughter will make the decisions. In many cases, when a daughter becomes out of control, a wrong choice is the root of the problem.

Recently a man admitted this was true in his home. The daughter first chose the wrong object for her affections, then lost respect for parental authority (they objected to her young man), and subsequently lost respect for all authority. Responsibility for her actions is clearly her own. In a related area, Proverbs deals specifically with sexual promiscuity by admonishing young men to stay away from prostitutes (chapters 5 and 7).

Stay away from drink

"Stay away from drink" is another admonition to the young. In a rather vivid account of the effects of alcohol the young man is told about the life of a drunkard. The passage in Proverbs 23:29-35 is particularly explicit in the Living Bible. The young are told about the hallucinations and delirium tremens as well as the silly things they are apt to say while intoxicated.

Through exposure to a close relative who was an alcoholic, my husband learned firsthand of its accompanying miseries. He was still a young man, and he determined then that if he never took the first drink he would never have the problem.

We have found the subject of liquor to be a sensitive one in many circles. Some churches have never considered it an evil to be avoided. Some which have traditionally avoided it are now taking the soft approach. Some believe Old Testament wine was not fermented. Others are sure it was. European Christians often partake of minimal amounts of wine with their meals.

Once in a small Italian town, my husband and I and two of our daughters dined at a little country inn with a local pastor and his wife. The host pastor asked if we would care for wine with our meal. My husband politely refused and our interpreter friend explained to our host that many evangelicals in America are total abstainers. Through the interpreter my husband then explained why he, personally, is a total abstainer.

The purpose here is not to discuss the final decision on the right or wrong of alcoholic beverages. The purpose is to show that this is one of the many areas over which parents cannot exercise complete control.

There are many parents who serve liquor to their minor children. On a transatlantic flight I saw a couple with their fifteen-year-old daughter being served by the flight attendant. When offered champagne, the mother refused, the father accepted and asked for one for the daughter. The attendant refused to serve her. The father protested, "She is allowed to drink at home."

The attendant was firm and tried to explain that it was a legal matter. It was settled to everyone's satisfaction when the mother decided that she, after all, would have a glass of champagne. After being served, she promptly went to sleep without touching her glass. The father and the daughter drank the champagne.

It is unfortunate that some parents of this persuasion also serve liquor to the friends of their minor children. The serving of liquor to minors at teenage parties has become a great problem in many communities. Parents who conscientiously try to screen all the activities of their teens are sometimes quite unaware that liquor is so available to minors. Even for those who are aware of the problem, it is difficult to deal with because the source of the liquor is usually a well-kept secret.

When our daughters were still in school, we knew that somewhere among the parents of their peers liquor was available to minors, but we had not one clue as to which home was involved. It was not until they had been out of school for several years that we learned the source. The information came quite by accident and, typically, it was the very last home we would have suspected. We never had reason to believe that our girls were using alcohol, but we lived with the knowledge that it was available and that they alone could control their actions in the matter. It is highly significant that the warning about liquor is given to the young. Parents cannot control the youth 100 percent of the time.

3. Accountability of the youth

The fact that the responsibility for actions is put upon the young is further delineated in passages which speak of strong judgment on the rebellious young. "God puts out the light of the man who curses his father or mother" (20:20, TLB). In the same vein, 30:17 declares: "A man who mocks his father and despises his mother shall have his eye plucked out by ravens and eaten by vultures" (TLB). This intimates an untimely death and reminds us that the first commandment with promise is to honor one's parents that one's days may be long upon the earth.

4. Unmerited suffering of the parents

Two similar passages, 27:11 and 23:15,16, further indicate that the child-learner is vested with much more responsibility than the parent-teacher. Here the father speaks to the son declaring how happy he will be *if* his son turns out to be a sensible man. The son who becomes a man of good sense is a public honor to the father. The father of a godly man has cause for joy. The wise son is a source of pleasure and the son is admonished to give his parents joy.

There can be no doubt that the unmerited suffering which the parent of a rebel endures is said to be the fault of the rebel, not of the parental training. The father of a level-headed son is happy, but the mother of a rebel is very sad (10:1; 15:20). The rebel is described as proud beyond description, arrogant, disdainful, and one who feels himself to be faultless despite his many sins and despite his cursing his mother and father (30:11,12).

5. Dealing with the rebel

Some specific observations about the rebel concern his lack of ambition, his unwillingness to receive correction, and his negative effect upon his family. Perhaps one of the most sobering thoughts concerning the rebel is found in 11:29 which states that "a fool who provokes his family to anger and resentment will finally have nothing worthwhile left" (TLB).

We see what we are not to do in dealing with the rebel. *Don't try to honor a rebel. T*o honor a rebel is like tying a stone to a slingshot; it will backfire (26:8). How often we have seen people who would cure rebellion in this manner! And don't expect talking to cure the rebel.

Talking to a rebel is usually useless. He will misapply an illustration and fail to get the point (26:9).

Don't argue with the rebel. That only makes one as foolish as the rebel. Proverbs 22:6 does tell us to train up a child in the way he should go and when he is old he will not depart from it. Verse 29:17 also promises that if you discipline your son he will give you happiness and peace of mind. Yet these verses must be balanced with 30:11 which states there are those who curse their father and mother, and with 12:1 which declares: "To learn you must want to be taught" (TLB).

The same book which tells parents to train a child also tells parents *not to waste time* on a rebel *or money* on one who does not want to learn (17:16). In fact, according to 22:10, if you would be rid of tension, fighting and quarrels, you must *throw the mocker out.*

To come to that point does not mean that the parent has necessarily failed. People who blame parents for the rebellious actions of a twenty-year-old are assuming that parental training means parental control, even over offspring who are legally of age.

Proverbs clearly holds the parent responsible to train children. Just as clearly, the book holds the youth responsible for many of his actions. If we are to discuss the theological implications of rebellion, then we must examine more than one isolated verse. We must balance Scripture with Scripture. It is theologically inconsistent to say that Proverbs 22:6 guarantees that a child will never rebel so long as he has received proper parental training. To apply this verse so universally and without regard to circumstances is to render the rest of the book of Proverbs meaningless.

PARENTAL PROJECT

Setting Standards

PROJECT: WORKING WEEKEND FOR PARENTS

- Get away if possible.
- Take along plenty of paper, pencils (include a red one) and a cooperative spirit.
- Set aside a definite time to work. Plan to follow the working period with a walk, a swim, dinner out, etc.

Discussion Time #1

Begin by discussing the value of standards to you and to your child. Try to isolate why you and your mate feel you should have any standards. (If you find that your goal is to control your child's behavior pattern for life, better reread chapter 2.) Try to determine how extensive your standards should be. For example, one theory on standards is, "We don't make many rules, but the ones we make are to be obeyed." Whether you agree with this or not, try to state your theory as clearly.

Work Time

Working separately, list what you consider to be proper standards. Then compare lists *without comment.* Proceed to develop a common standard in this manner:

1. Underline in red all those items which both of you listed.
2. Place a red check beside those which are only on one list but with which you essentially agree.
3. Place a red question mark beside all others.

Discussion Time #2

Begin with statements with red checks. Discuss them one by one until you have covered statements on both lists. Does your mate feel you should modify some statements? Define them more clearly? When you have agreed on the final form of all checked statements, you are ready to tackle those statements marked with a red question mark, but you may wish to take a break before you do.

Discussion Time #3

These may be harder to manage. Keep the tone of your discussion civil. Let the one who proposed the statement explain *all* the reasons behind it. Make your final decision on the statement on one of these three levels:

1. You're absolutely right. I just didn't think of it.

2. I don't feel as strongly about it, but I believe you are right.

3. I don't agree with you all the way, but I'll stand with you all the way.

If you reach an impasse—you cannot use one of the above and the parent who proposed the statement is not convinced you should drop it—go on to the next statement. Take some time to think. Come back to it. Remember, the object of the project is to find a standard upon which you can mutually agree.

PART THREE

Revising Standards for the Wrong Reasons

4

Politics, Peers and Parental Pressures

Experts constantly question the standards parents set, as do neighbors, the children, and even the parents themselves. Parents should not depend on support of their standards as a verification of the need for demanding them. Someone will always be around to challenge what the parent is trying to do. It is easy to lose perspective under a barrage of criticism, and parents become so confused that they sometimes revise their standards for the wrong reasons. They begin to wonder, "Do I have the right to demand this of my child?" or, "Should I make some drastic revisions in my standards?"

Revising standards for the wrong reasons

One friend asked, "Should we insist our youth cling to our old morals or should we just roll with the punches? If we roll, how far shall we roll?"

A parent in this quandary should ask himself, "Why am I considering rolling with the punches?" (Or, "Why am I adamantly refusing to do so?")

"Am I giving in simply because I think it will give my child less *reason* to rebel?" (Or, "Am I refusing to budge because I think it will give him less *room* to rebel?")

In other words, is the decision being made in order to find a way to control Johnny better or to control him for a longer time?

When parents begin to question their own standards, it is usually because they are looking at those standards from Johnny's perspective. They begin to wonder how Johnny will react. I would advise parents in this position to move very cautiously. Don't change standards which you believe to be right in the hope of gaining more control over Johnny. You may be disappointed.

Certainly I do not advocate rigidity, but a parent does have the right to set standards which he believes to be right, whether or not Johnny accepts those standards. To begin reversing, lowering, or changing those standards in an effort to control the child usually results in only one thing: While trying to maintain control over the child's life, the parent loses control over his own. If this happens and Johnny still rebels, what does the parent have left?

Admittedly, setting standards can be a problem, but it should not become more complicated because the parent is looking at it from Johnny's perspective rather than his own. A parent has the right to set standards with which he is comfortable. So long as he is responsible for Johnny, he has the right to demand certain things of Johnny.

Biblically based standards questioned

We made our own standard of child-rearing as biblically based as we could. I strongly advocate this for every parent. We can expect any biblical principles which deal with human relationships to be good, sound principles. After all, who knows more about human nature than the God who made us?

We arrived at our standard out of personal conviction—not because we felt it necessary to maintain a certain image since my husband is a minister. We never had a double standard (one for home and one for the congregation to see). In fact, we let our girls know that our standards had nothing to do with their father being a minister. We would have had the same standards no matter what profession he followed.

As a mother, I also tried to have an understanding with our congregations. I have never objected to other adults correcting my children. (I have, on occasion, corrected children other than my own.) However, my one request was that it never be done on the basis of, "You are the minister's daughter; you ought to know better." Rather, I preferred they simply say, "You should not do that"; or, "You're old enough to know better." To my knowledge, no one in our congregations ever disappointed me in that respect.

Time for change?

Increasingly, Christian standards are threatened by the moral pressures of our age. Questions are raised repeatedly. Can biblical principles provide a basis for meeting the pressures and problems of the twentieth century? Can the younger generation relate to Christian principles? Can our churches meet the continuing needs of today's youth?

Under the pressure of these issues we see teens rebel, parents panic and churches flounder. We also notice that solutions multiply. Everyone wants to make faith work, and we all want to write the rules. The theologian declares it's time to change the message; the innovative youth pastor says we must change the methods; the Sunday school curriculum editor insists that it is once again time to revise the revisions!

Change is all around. Traditional worship services have been replaced by new formats, and music has taken on a new sound. I will concur that some change is necessary, but change in the program does little to make Christian principles more palatable. Parents continue to face a never-ending struggle to relate those principles to their children.

Last night's news telecast, today's newspaper, this week's news magazine — all bring details of current confusion concerning moral standards. The courts and the medical profession repeatedly argue what is right or wrong with abortion, infanticide and genocide. Advances in the world of medicine have created a terrifying limbo in which we can keep a man alive but cannot make him well. The old are forbidden to die and the unborn refused the right to live. Man and woman have long since won the right to live together without a marriage license. Increasingly, man and man are demanding the right to live together with a proper marriage license.

The reminders of the moral pressures of the twentieth century are always with us. Our sensitivities are shocked, and it is natural to assume that, since the moral confusion is so great today, parents should revise the standards to accommodate peer pressures on their teenagers.

To those who feel that Christian standards are unrealistic, I'd like to point out this fact: If world conditions ever had constituted a legitimate excuse to give up personal standards, Christianity would have died in its first generation. The problem of Christian living in a non-christian world is as old as Christianity itself.

Moral confusion

Christianity was born into a sick and dying society. Witches, pornography, obscene theater, violent entertainment, prostitution, formal contracts between homosexuals—such was the insanity of the world into which Christianity came. Divorce was granted either party with almost no contest. Men curled their hair and their long flowing beards. According to Will Durant, it was an age which produced men of intellect without morals, abilities without scruples, and courage without honor.[1]

As a Christian mother, I do not believe God is taken by surprise. I believe He made full provision for every pressure of every generation. He laid down the principles for handling the "new" morality on its first time around nearly two thousand years ago when it was no more than the old Roman immorality.

Through the apostle Paul, God warned the early Christians to separate themselves from the standards (or lack of them) in the world around them (2 Corinthians 6:17). Constantly, these early believers were challenged to a higher moral standard. God never said it would be easy. He simply said this is the way a believer should live. Since that time every generation has had to face its own set of moral problems and pressures.

Withstanding pressures

Whether or not the standards you have set for your home are biblically based, I believe this rule applies: If you have set a standard which you believe to be correct, don't revise it just because the moral pressures of the age are so great. If parents look for easy solutions, it is not likely they will be able to set any personal standards for the home.

Lest anyone think I am advocating that parents completely ignore their teenager's feelings about standards, let me state what I believe to be an important principle: A parent should develop the ability to listen sympathetically without condoning a questionable action. It is one thing to deal with Johnny's problem in accordance with your standards. It is quite another to hysterically tell Johnny that he shouldn't have the problem. Obviously, he does have it.

The parent should listen, but there will be times when the parent must close the conversation with a firm but sympathetic conclusion: "I may be wrong, but so long as I am responsible for you, that will be my decision."

Once, I overheard a mother of our community commenting on an incident which took place while her son was in high school. His parents had cautioned him not to take the family car to a certain place because the road was torn up and would be rough on the tires. Not only did he take the car anyway, but he also completely ruined a tire in the process. His mother told him he would forfeit the use of the car until he had earned enough money to pay for the tire she had to replace.

"But Mom," he wailed, "I have a date tonight."

"Then you had better go into the house and call her and explain that you have no car," she told her son.

I admire her objectivity, but the point which really interested me was what she said next. A neighbor man was on the scene and heard it all. When the son was out of earshot he said, "You're hard on him. For two cents

I'd give him the keys to my Cadillac for tonight."

The mother told her neighbor that if he ever did such a thing he would have her to contend with, and that so long as she was responsible for her son, she would discipline him as she saw fit.

This incident reminded me of another problem parents face in maintaining personal standards for the home—that of constant interference from outside the home. Neighbors, relatives, schools and legal agencies are all guilty of criticizing parents for the standards those parents impose on their own children. I think this mother did a wise thing when she let the neighbor know how she felt. Too many times a parent allows this type of pressure to confuse the issue at hand.

Sometimes outside pressure takes a more subtle form. I recall one period when one of our teenage daughters had developed a close friendship with another girl whose parents held standards similar to ours. Before long I noticed that when my daughter asked if she and Cindy could do something together, she always worded it the same way. "Cindy's mom said whatever you decided was okay. If I can go, she can go."

As time went along I continued to get the same question, even when I was sure that Cindy's mother would not approve of what our daughters were planning. Finally I called her and asked her opinion of the latest plan.

"Oh, no," she said, "I don't want Cindy to do that, but I was sure you would say no, so I just told Cindy that whatever you decided would be okay."

I pointed out to her that, because she was avoiding her responsibility, my relationship was being severely strained with both girls. Fortunately, we were good friends and she immediately corrected her error. I never had to deal with that problem again.

Special problems concerning minors

Although we have never faced the problem of a minor out of control, I have seen many parents in our churches who have. Contrary to what some believe, I do not believe the parents are usually to blame. I am overwhelmed at the complexity of the problems created by a minor out of control. I am appalled at the interference with which the parents must contend when they attempt to deal with their child.

Now, I would not for a minute question the existence of abused and battered children in our country who are the helpless victims of sick parents. Nor would I deny there are teenage girls who are sexually molested by their stepfathers or biological fathers. However, we have seen the other side also.

Some children have an uncanny way of convincing the neighbors, the school counselors, and even the juvenile courts that they are being misunderstood and mistreated, when this is not the case. A subtle form of blackmail develops as soon as the child learns that there are those who will listen to him, and that as yet his parents have not discovered where to tell their side of the story.

We have seen the sheer frustration of parents who know they have a child out of control, yet they cannot get anyone to listen. We have seen the thirteen-year-old girls who cry rape, accusing fathers, brothers, stepfathers and stepbrothers, when in fact it was not the case.

We have seen thirteen-year-olds involve two sets of parents and the juvenile court in an endless argument over who should be in charge, simply by accusing one of the parents of cruelty. Of course in time the truth comes out and the parents are absolved. In the meantime, though, the parents have lived a nightmarish existence.

Strangely, their primary concern is never for their own reputation which surely is at stake. Rather, their real concern is for their child who is out of control but who still manages to control the situation. These parents know that their child will, in the end, lose more than anyone else.

One frustrating case we observed was that of a girl, age 15 (going on 30), who kept the entire family in a turmoil. She developed a very serious relationship with a nineteen-year-old young man who was out of school. Everything possible was done to keep the daughter from dating or seeing the young man, but, as is often the case, it was to no avail. Eventually the daughter told her mother she wanted to marry the young man. Of course the parents refused. The daughter then threatened to go to the birth control clinic to get the pill. If they couldn't get married, at least they could sleep together.

After thinking it over, the mother decided that perhaps a teenage marriage was the better solution. She relented and gave her consent. The crowning blow came when she discovered that while it was completely legal for her fifteen-year-old to obtain the pill without parental consent, it was legally impossible for her to get married even with parental consent. In her state there is a minimum age law for marriage, but none for receiving contraceptives at the birth control clinic.

Laws concerning minors and their parents can be both confusing and frustrating. Perhaps more parents need to become politically active in matters which concern minors.

It is difficult to be legally responsible for someone whom you cannot legally control—but the responsible person should be the one to control the decision.

While discussing this subject, one mother said that she had refused to allow her son to participate in a certain high school activity. She believed it to be too dangerous.

"So long as I have to pay your doctor bills, I will have to forbid you to do that," she told her son.

While I might not have made the same decision, I agree 100 percent with her reasoning and her right to make the decision. It is a principle which we should endeavor to carry out at all levels, whether decisions are being challenged by our children, our peers, or our government agencies.

Factors which prevent satisfactory solutions

The times in which we live complicate the problems of parenthood, but the root of the problem is not the moral pressures in themselves. As pointed out earlier, every pressure this generation feels, some generation in the past felt also.

There are two factors which make our times different.

The **first** is the legal interference in the home. Someone outside the home dictates what is right for the child but assumes no responsibility for the child.

The **second** is the prolonged period of adolescence in which a child demands all his rights but assumes no responsibility.

Until something is done about these two factors, parents will continue to face some problems for which there are no satisfactory solutions.

Changing standards will not guarantee control over minors

Parents in the past few decades have openly expressed concern about the issue of control. A 1973 *Better Homes and Gardens* magazine contained an enlightening article, "What's Happening to the American Family?" The author polled parents on two questions: (1) At what age do parents lose control? and (2) At what age should parents relinquish control?

Amazingly, the answers showed that the majority of parents believe they are losing control long before they should. Sixty percent of the parents polled believe they should relinquish control when the child is between the ages of 19 and 21. This would indicate that many parents believe they should maintain control until the child is of age. In spite of what they believe is right, though, 54 percent of those same parents believe that teenagers are out of control today before they are 15. Of that number, 24 percent stated that the child is out of control before the age of 13.[2]

Maybe you are a parent with a minor out of control. I would not attempt to give you some simplistic solution for your complicated problem, but I do encourage you to try to keep your perspective. If you have carefully thought out a standard for your home, don't change it because your child has learned to manipulate everyone around, or because the local birth control clinic dispenses pills on demand. Remember that you do not set your standard on the basis of whether or not everyone will adhere to it. You set it because it is right. If Johnny refuses to obey, don't change the standard; keep trying to change Johnny.

Finally, a word to those who may not have a personal relationship with Jesus Christ. I have a list of things in life which I would hate to go through without the Lord, and being a mother of teenagers tops the list. I could not have survived those years without Him. May I encourage you to put your faith and trust in Him. Even when you cannot satisfactorily control your child's life, you can find personal comfort if you will pray, "Lord, take control of my life."

* * * * *

These materials will give you further help in how to receive Christ and how to experience the abundant life He has promised:

"The Four Spiritual Laws,"
a booklet published by
Campus Crusade for Christ, Int.,
will guide you step by step toward
putting your faith in Christ.

"Would You Like to Know God Personally?"
is a new and updated adaptation of
"The Four Spiritual Laws" booklet.

The First Year of Your Christian Life,
by Steven L. Pogue, will help you
get started on the right track
in your Christian life.

All are available at Christian bookstores everywhere, or you may call Here's Life Publishers at

1-800-950-4HLP.

5

Perpetuating Parental Values in the Home

In considering parental problems with standards, we have examined two general areas: setting standards for the wrong reasons, and revising standards for the wrong reasons. In the latter segment there is one final problem we should consider. It is that of relinquishing control of adult offspring.

The parent must recognize that as an adult Johnny has the right to develop standards which differ from those of his parents. At the same time, though, the parents should not revise the standards of the home to accommodate Johnny's chosen lifestyle.

Reflecting parental values in the lifestyle of the home

The parent must differentiate between controlling the lifestyle of the home and controlling the offspring for life. For example, Johnny takes an off-campus apartment at college and rooms with his girlfriend. He wants to continue his living arrangements during a weekend visit to the parent's home. He may even apply pressure on his parents by using such logic as, "It would be hypocritical to have different rooms at home when we share the same bed every night."

The issue becomes very confused as parents and son are drawn into an argument over who has the right to determine the moral habits of an adult son.

The parents declare, "We'll never approve."

Johnny counters with, "I'm of age."

To settle the issue many parents find it necessary to send an SOS to Ann Landers or Dear Abby asking, "What shall we do?"

The real issue involved in the weekend visit question is not, "Who controls Johnny's morals?" Obviously, he has already settled that question to his own satisfaction. The issue is, "Who controls the lifestyle of the home?"

It is not a matter of the parents saying, "Johnny, we will not allow you to live this way." It is a matter of saying, "Johnny, we will not allow this in our home." It is the right of the parent to determine what goes on in the home.

Some time ago, in *Today's Health,* one writer expressed it thus: "Parents should make their reservations clear if they have them. That is, if they do not condone sleeping together outside of marriage, they must not allow this in their home."[1] Johnny may go through years of fighting parental values. These years will be a time of confusion and clouded issues if the parents fail to follow this principle.

The standards which determine the lifestyle of the home should reflect the values of the parents. From the beginning, parents will develop guidelines which reflect their values. This is not something they consciously decide, and it is natural to train young toddlers out of the background of one's own set of values. Only as the children grow and challenge those guidelines does it become necessary to define parental values more clearly.

It is not my purpose to tell you what those values should be. Instead I want to emphasize that, whether being developed or being revised, guidelines should always reflect parental values.

Maintaining control of the lifestyle of the home

Controlling the lifestyle of the home is not the same as controlling the offspring for life. While the parents have a responsibility to control minor children, their chief responsibility toward adult offspring is to counsel. Parents cannot apply rules made for fifteen-year-olds to adult offspring. To do so only antagonizes and alienates these older children. However, a parent may apply rules for what goes on in his own home—regardless of the age of the children. There is a difference in trying to tell Johnny how to live and in telling him what is permissible in the parental home.

Many of the statements in this book concern adult offspring and would not be applicable to minor children. Certainly a twenty-one-year-old son who is tearing the family apart should be handled differently than a fifteen-year-old son who is doing the same. On the other hand, a twenty-one-year-old son who is living in harmony at home should expect to have more freedom than his fifteen-year-old brother.

It is surprising how easily so many parents lose this perspective. They find it difficult to make a variation in the rules for separate age groups, and they completely fail to see that some rules should be perpetuated regardless of the age group. Parents have the right to impose behavioral standards in their own home. These standards are not subject to vote or to veto by offspring who refuse to accept parental standards.

Distinct age groups versus family democracy

Outside forces often cloud parental perspective concerning age groups within the home. When our children were growing up, one of the popular issues was "togetherness." The age groups within the home were ignored. Even the distinction between parent and child was minimized. Supposedly this avoided fragmenting the family. Not only did the experts suggest that the family do everything together, but they also strongly advised that children sit in on most of the decisions. Almost without realizing it, many parents came to view the ideal family as a democratically run unit.

In theory it sounded good and I suspect it sold a lot of magazines during those years, but in practice it didn't work. (Theories which portray children and adults functioning as equals seldom prove workable.)

Like other parents, I am sometimes subconsciously influenced by current trends. I found myself trying to apply some of those togetherness theories to the decision-making process in our home. It could hardly be described as a successful venture.

I recall attending a seminar for parents in which we were discussing family planning for family happenings. Somewhat frustrated, I asked the leader how one might discover something the entire family would enjoy. I explained that I was conscious of the fleeting years and wanted to do things with my children which would count for the years ahead. Specifically, I wanted to be able to go to bed at night knowing that "today we created a memory." With everyone in on the planning session, though, nothing was getting done. What appealed to one child was boring with a capital *"B"* to the others.

One woman, whose children were grown, responded to my question with a simple statement. "I do not remember ever asking my children if they wanted to go on a picnic," she said. "When my husband and I decided we had the time, and the children had the need for a picnic, I simply packed a basket and we took them."

Since that day I have made many additional discoveries which underscore her theory. A former classmate from high school days went with her husband and two young children on an extended cruise in their sailboat. Although they had not initially planned it that way, they eventually sailed from the Virgin Islands through the Panama Canal and home to the Port of San Diego. In describing the experience to the local press afterward, Peggy laughingly remarked, "At no time were the children in favor of this cruise. Not at the beginning, not at the end, and at no time in the middle." Of course, when it was over they were glad for the experience.

The point is, whether it is a simple picnic or an exciting round-the-world cruise, if it is purely a democratic decision, chances are that no memories will be made. Certainly there is a need for a creative means to train children in the decision-making process, but to strive for total democracy as a family is ludicrous.

Weaknesses of the democratic process would be a very minor problem if confined to such questions as what to do for family recreation. The topic would have very little to do with the subject matter of this book. However, parents who think of the family as a democratic unit when deciding on vacations also usually try to handle their problems by some type of democratic process. By the time Johnny reaches the prime age for rebellion, the parents are convinced they do not have the right to impose their values upon him.

The democratic process should never be employed to determine or control the lifestyle of the home. Such decisions are the responsibility of the parents alone. The minor child fits into the lifestyle primarily through the aid of rules which the parents lay down for him to obey. The adult offspring living at home fits into that lifestyle primarily out of respect for his parents.

From rules to respect

When our daughters were growing up, they always had a curfew. In the beginning they knew only one thing about that curfew. They had to come home at a certain hour because their parents believed they were too young to be out any later. It did not matter what time their friends went home. It did not matter that they did not agree with us about the curfew 100 percent of the time. Parental valued determined their curfew. They obeyed the curfew because we punished them if they failed to meet it.

However, it was interesting to see how they each continued to honor this curfew as they grew older. Each of them lived at home for a while after they were of age. Two of them lived at home throughout a lengthy engagement period. During their adult years at home we made no conscious attempt to force them to keep a curfew, but they each honored it. They kept it, or they made prior arrangements for an anticipated late date, or they apologized when something unexpected detained them. They did not do this because they were too young to decide when to come in but out of respect for us.

Just before moving away, our youngest daughter discussed the curfew issue with a friend. The other girl was having quite a struggle with her parents over the late hours (early morning, to be exact) she was keeping. Because she was of age, she felt her parents should not try to tell her how to live.

Our daughter said to her, "I'm a year older than you and I still wouldn't think of keeping those kinds of hours. So long as you're living at home, you have to remember that parents worry a lot. They lose too much sleep if you stay out so late."

The elusive goal

The key to prevention of rebellion continues to be the most sought-after goal of millions of parents. It is, and will continue to be, an elusive goal. No one can tell you how to raise your child in such a way that you will never have to cope with his rebellion. There are no success formulas — only success stories.

During my research for this book, I discussed this topic with a young friend. She cited several middle-aged couples with whom she and her husband are intimately acquainted and whom they admire. These couples are facing problems with their teenagers. My friend is supportive of the parents and their child-rearing methods. She does not view their present crises as an indication of parental failure. She believes these parents have done everything required of them, and more. Yet their teens are rebelling against parental values.

The experience of these parents has affected my friend deeply. Yet childless, she confided in me two reasons for remaining so. One is the nature of her husband's work, and the other is that neither she nor her husband feel emotionally prepared to risk the heartbreak which their friends are experiencing.

Through our conversations, as well as through my own observations, I notice that my friend is criticized for her childless state by people who paint rosy pictures of the joys of parenthood. When she voiced her concern over this I encouraged her to remember it is a private decision and she should not allow pressures from insensitive outsiders to affect her.

Then I reminded her that in life every situation has a set of joys and a set of heartaches. Certainly there are joys peculiar only to parenthood which she will never experience. On the other hand, there are some heartaches which come with the territory. These she will escape. Only the idealist paints parenthood as all fun and games. Only the cynic declares it to be nothing but pain.

When children pass through the teenage years into young adulthood, parenthood becomes characterized by confusion. Confusion over when to change parental standards is a perpetual problem. If a parent finds it necessary to revise his standards, it should be because of personal conviction. Parents may find it easier to control a minor child than to relinquish control of an adult offspring, but parents must never relinquish control of the lifestyle of the home.

It is their home.

It must reflect their values.

PARENTAL PROJECT

Revising Standards

PROJECT: WORKING WEEKEND FOR PARENTS

- In preparing for the weekend, follow the same instructions as for the first parental project.

Discussion Time

Since this project is to discuss the need for revising (or refusing to revise) parental standards, it is assumed the parents have a definite standard upon which they previously have agreed. In discussing the possibility of revising parental standards, apply the following question to every statement or guideline which makes up your agreed-upon standard for the home:

**"When should we amend or
rescind this statement?"**

Answer with one of the following:

1. Never. It is too basic to our sense of right and wrong.
2. When Johnny is 16, old enough to drive and to assume some responsibility.
3. If Johnny is still living at home after he is of age.

Work Time

Do a quick final check on your mutual standard. On the basis of your discussion concerning revisions, you should now have standards which you can divide into the following three basic categories:

A. We foresee no circumstance which would cause us to change our opinion on this. Our children will adhere to it.

B. We cannot foresee that we would change our opinion, but we will allow Johnny to make his own decision at age _____.

C. This represents the chosen lifestyle of our home. Even adult offspring living at home must adhere to this.

As you revise your standards, make sure you are clear on the difference between controlling the lifestyle of the home and controlling your child for life.

* * * * *

Additional reading suggestions:

Pulling Weeds, Planting Seeds: Growing Character in Your Life and Family,
by Dennis Rainey

Why Teens Are Killing Themselves,
by Marion Duckworth

Talking With Your Kids About Love, Sex and Dating,
by Barry and Carol St. Clair

Surviving the Tweenage Years,
by Gary and Angela Hunt

And for your children:

The Handling Your Hassles Series, including *Friendships, Self-Image, Temptation, What's On Your Mind?, Parents,* and *Peer Pressure,*
by Bill Jones

All are available at Christian bookstores, or you may call Here's Life Publishers at 1-800-950-4HLP.

PART FOUR

The Parents
Face a Casualty

6

Emergency Procedures for Coping With an Immediate Crisis

If the roof suddenly fell in and destroyed your home, how long would you stand amidst the rubble asking, "Why did this happen?" before you began to ask, "What am I going to do?"

Often I have seen pictures of families standing in the ruins of their home which has been destroyed by some catastrophe. Invariably, these people, while still in an obvious state of shock, are already picking through the debris trying to salvage something of what remains.

The constructive question

Where to begin is a big question, because there is nothing orderly about a house with the roof fallen in. Not only are contents damaged or destroyed, but everything is shoved around in the crash. Hopeless as it may appear, one thing is certain. Before the residents can begin any reconstruction, they must sort out, discard, salvage or haul away the debris. It is there one must begin. One piece or one load at a time.

How similar this is to the scene a parent confronts immediately after a crisis which threatens to disintegrate the family. When our lives cave in because of the actions of a son or daughter, everything seems to be a jumbled, disorderly, chaotic mess. Standing amid the shambles of our private emotions and our corporate family life, we wonder how we will ever reconstruct anything meaningful.

There is one basic similarity between reconstructing a caved-in life and reconstructing a caved-in house. In either case, the longer one remains in the limbo of "Why did it happen?" the longer he puts off the reconstruction process.

"What am I going to do about it?" is a far more constructive question.

The people involved

If you are trying to put your life back together after the rebellion of an offspring, the first area to consider is that of the people involved. You. Your mate. The children yet at home. The son or daughter responsible. I mention this individual last because once the crisis has come, once that person has made his choice, the focus should change to rebuilding the family life for those who remain. You can no longer put all your time and effort into trying to change the course Johnny is taking, or control him any longer, or prevent the inevitable mess he is making of his life.

Let's begin with yourself. You may experience one of several emotions. Numbness and detachment. Despair. Anger. Resentment. Whatever the feeling, its force is likely to be so great that it will be debilitating. Merely functioning will demand strenuous effort on your part. Getting through the necessary daily routine will require determination. At this crucial state, that goal is enough. Get through the day, one hour at a time. This is not a good time to try to find solutions for problems the future is certain to hold. Concentrate on solving the immediate problems of each hour.

At such a time as this, the Christian parent should learn to lean on the Lord Jesus Christ. The temptation is to say, "Lord, if I could just understand, it wouldn't hurt so much!" The need, though, is to pray, "Lord, I know You promised peace that passeth understanding [Philippians 4:7], and I need that right now."

It is important, even while you are still in need of comfort, that you make an effort to give comfort to those who share your sorrow. Your mate must have some loving attention because each of you suffers and each of you has needs. Obviously, you need each other in a very special way when you are facing a common heartache. You must reach out and be sensitive to each other's ache. You must reach out and be sensitive to each other's suffering. Grief can quickly drown you if you think only of yourself.

Extremes to avoid

There are two extremes to avoid in any suffering. **One** is trying to be too brave and never allowing yourself to give in to the emotional upheaval you feel. Years of pent-up grief will do strange things to people physically, emotionally and spiritually.

The **other** extreme to avoid is that of making a lifelong hobby of your suffering. Even in the very beginning of your suffering, you must shift the focus and force yourself to see that there are others who stand beside you and ache as you ache. You need not mouth a lot of superficial phrases promising rosy tomorrows which you do not foresee, nor do you need to say things you do not yet believe. Do force yourself, though, to see that you are not the only one who is hurting. This will help you give a quiet "I love you" at the right time or a simple, encouraging "We'll make it, honey." It shows the other person you care.

You also must make a special effort to help the children yet in the home. Teenagers are likely to go into a tailspin. If Johnny was the oldest, and his siblings looked up to him, those siblings will have special problems. Linda was the younger of two children. She had always compared herself unfavorably with her brother in spite of her parents' efforts to counteract this. She wanted to achieve everything he achieved in life because she felt obligated to do so. He always did everything right, was seldom in trouble at home and never in trouble out of the home. She would, at times, convince herself that she was a second-class citizen because she couldn't live up to this self-imposed goal to be like her brother.

When he was twenty-one, her brother suddenly decided he wanted a completely different lifestyle. Just before the holidays he packed a small suitcase and left his wife, telling her not to bother to look for him. He was going to San Francisco and when he was ready to see anyone from the family he would let them know. There was an angry scene in which the parents tried to reason with him, but to no avail.

"For once I'm going to do what I want to do," he said and off he went.

The entire family felt torn apart, but Linda was hit especially hard. Suddenly her model had disappeared.

This brother whom she had felt so compelled to copy was no longer worth it.

Linda was angry. She was even panic-stricken. She made a lot of irreversible decisions during that period of her life because she felt, *If my brother couldn't make it, what chance do I have?*

She broke off a serious relationship with her boyfriend, and, for the first time, she experimented with alcohol. She was still a minor. She went out one night to a friend's home and got drunk.

Finding ways to help

While Linda's parents tightened up their supervision and were very firm about what they expected from her, they also tried to find ways to help her through the difficult period. They especially tried to find ways to show her that she was important to them as a person. They realized that she was going through a very confusing time trying to sort out her feelings.

Finding ways to help is important at this stage. At any given moment one family member will be experiencing more difficulty than the others. This is not to say that it will be easy for anyone, but because emotions vary, a different person will be the one having the most difficulty on succeeding days. Whichever person it is will need the encouragement of everyone else in the family at that time.

I recall a period of extreme difficulty in our own family during which we were all having a hard time coping. One day my husband found it especially hard getting from one moment to the next. One of our daughters just sat down beside him for a few minutes. With a gentle nudge in the ribs she said very quietly, "Oh, Dad, it'll be okay." That was all he needed to get him through that day.

One very practical way to aid everyone in getting through the "debris" period is to go out as a family for a meal. At home there is nothing to keep you from giving in to your emotions 24 hours a day. When you go out for a meal, though, or to some public function, you normally expect to maintain control over your emotions. You will be forced to call a moratorium on your problem for a few hours. While those hours spent together may not be altogether joyous, they will provide a much needed diversion.

Perceived interference

One difficult problem parents face in the initial crisis is the relationship with the rebelling child. Johnny will not be thinking rationally; therefore, it will be nearly impossible to predict his reactions to anything you say or do.

Robert had given his parents an especially hard time. At nineteen he declared his right to leave home, and he took an apartment with his girlfriend. He made it very clear he wanted no interference from his family. Certainly he didn't want them to try to locate him, although he was remaining in the same city. Yet within a week he had informed his sixteen-year-old brother that his parents obviously cared nothing for him. They had made no effort to see him at the service station where he worked.

Any contact made in a situation like this may be interpreted as interference. Yet no contact at all can be seen as a lack of love. The rebelling son or daughter will even begin to blame the family because the new relationship with the family makes him feel like a stranger.

In Robert's case, as he began to feel left out, he

poured out his feelings to one of his peers. The friend happened to be the son of old family friends. Having heard only one side of the story this family soon contacted Robert's parents to intercede for him.

"He feels you will not let him come home," they said. "Can't you reconsider and let him come back?"

Of course it surprised the well-meaning friends to learn that Robert, and not his parents, had demanded the new relationship which had left him feeling so alone.

"Leave me alone," uttered by an angry child in the hysterical beginnings of a full-scale rebellion must be taken with reservation. What the child is really wanting at that stage of his life is the best of two worlds, yours and his. To him that makes sense even if his parents know it is unreasonable, irrational and impossible.

A parent must move cautiously at this point. Don't try a lengthy lecture on irrational behavior. He will not comprehend it. On the other hand, don't give in to every whim Johnny has. Trying to do everything he seems to be telling you to do will reduce you to a puppet on a string. Remember, now that he has made the break and brought on a whole spectrum of family problems, you must think of yourself, your mate and your other children first. That means you will weigh every decision by how it will affect the rest of the family.

Establishing boundaries

You must see boundary lines clearly. All major decisions will fall into two categories: (1) "I may not approve, but it's your life, Johnny"; and (2) "You may not like it, but it's our home, Johnny."

The life that Johnny is bent on messing up for years to come is his to mess up—but that home which he persists in destroying in the process is yours to protect. If that means taking a hard line with Johnny, so be it.

Robert's parents came to two decisions soon after his break with the family. If Robert wanted to start living with a girl at his own expense, it was his life. If his parents did not want him to bring her home for a meal or a weekend, they had that right—it was their home. There was no need for them to allow things of which they did not approve to go on in their home.

This is a principle about which we have always been firm in our home. I believe it is something parents must begin to practice when children are very small if they expect to enforce it when a teenage crisis comes. For example, when our girls were small they knew that the children who came to play had to play by the rules of the house. When their friends jumped on the beds I always informed them, "Our girls are not allowed to do that, so as long as you are playing in their home, you cannot do it either."

Many people have a hard time making decisions of this nature, but it is an important principle for anyone who values his home as his own. I believe it affects many areas of your life, and the more you stick by that principle the easier it is to apply it in time of crisis.

As a small girl I watched how my parents entertained and how they visited. Through their example I learned that certain manners are observed by the host and hostess, and certain manners are observed by the guests in the home.

Through the years my husband and I have entertained all manner of guests in our home. Most of them I enjoyed immensely, but I remember one I did not enjoy. He was a stranger to us but was traveling with one of our good friends. In that capacity he was a dinner guest in our home. In a short while he began talking on a very controversial subject and spent the next several hours in an argumentative mood. As his hostess I was offended, not by his views which he certainly had a right to have, but by how he conducted himself as a guest in my home.

Needless to say, he was never invited back.

I still believe that one's home should be one's castle. No one, not even Johnny, should be allowed to force you to endure things in your home against your wishes. An estranged child seldom conducts himself as a family member. Neither does he behave as a guest. How does one handle an adult offspring who does not conduct himself properly in his parents' home?

Joe related to us how he handled the problem. His son had married very young, against the parents' wishes and advice. The son was so angry because his parents would not give their wholehearted approval that he refused to see them for more than two years. Finally, after the birth of the first grandchild, the young couple visited the parents. It was a terrible week for all of them. The daughter-in-law was sloppy, lazy and thoughtless. She barely took care of the baby. Observing none of the social rules for guests in a home, the couple took advantage of a complete vacation with sister and mother providing the maid service.

After the week was over, Joe called his son aside. "How you live your life is your business," he said, "but I will not tolerate unthoughtful conduct in our home. Until you can come back and assume your share of keeping things picked up and conduct yourself as something besides a freeloader, you will not be welcome."

Making social contact

A question many parents face is how to make social contact with their children, especially those involved in sexual misconduct. Robert's parents handled their situation in a manner with which they were comfortable. After a brief cooling-off period, they felt it was time to make some contact with their son. They did not wish to have him and his roommate come to their home, and even if Robert and his roommate had invited them to visit at their apartment, the parents did not wish to do that, either.

Instead, they chose a way in which they could have some time with Robert without appearing to condone his actions. They contacted him at work and arranged to take him to lunch. They spent an hour together eating and talking of everything except the issue which had driven them apart. After several such contacts, Robert began dropping by alone to visit his parents. Of course the relationship could hardly be expected to be the same. When a person must guard his conversation in order to avoid infringing on another's rights, the relationship remains superficial.

Learning to cope

Learning to cope is an essential part of being a parent. Watching people who have suffered and who have learned to cope with sorrow gives a parent courage when most needed. One of our friends from seminary days has seen more sorrow than anyone else of our acquaintance. When we first met, we had a year-old daughter. He and his wife had already lost one child and his wife was pregnant again. Since that time, he has lost another child, his wife, his mother and a sister. A singularly successful pastor and a much sought-after speaker, he seldom refers to his sufferings. He refuses to allow himself to dwell on that side of life because to do so would tap the energy he needs. However, on one occasion we were visiting after a space of many years and inevitably some of the incidents of the past surfaced. At the close of the visit I made a passing comment concerning our heartache over a daughter who was estranged at the time. Instantly, our friend was all sympathy. To him sorrow is sorrow. Whether through death or other circumstances, the loss of a child causes a great deal of suffering for a parent. It is because parents have no control over suffering that it becomes necessary to cope.

I have another friend whose ability to cope is an example worth mentioning. When her son was three years old he was found to be epileptic. Through the years he became progressively worse. I recall visiting with them when he was about ten, and my friend explained that the seizures could not be completely controlled and the medication was a problem. He was constantly under heavy sedation. There were other problems also. They faced some rather ugly facts of life along the way. They moved at least once because a neighborhood was not receptive to the afflicted son.

Early in her son's illness, my friend realized that a parent could react in one of two ways. She could stand among the debris of broken dreams and bitterly denounce God, fate, and the inadequacy of medical science, or she could find a way to cope. She decided to cope. She became involved in educating the public on epilepsy. The governor of her state appointed her to serve on a committee which deals with problems of epilepsy and other handicaps. Nothing she did could diminish her son's illness, but it heightened her ability to cope. So effective was that ability that I had forgotten that behind her beautiful, spontaneous smile my friend still suffered a great deal.

One week before his twentieth birthday, her son died in a home accident related to a seizure. We lived more than 300 miles away and it was some time before I learned of his death. When I did I called her. We talked briefly, then she said, "I know he is happy now. I know where he is and I know that no one is laughing at him any more."

In that moment I realized to what extent she had suffered as a mother, even while she coped. I was so moved I had to hang up. I couldn't talk anymore. Her hurt was there for 17 years, but she coped, and her life was better for it. Many others benefited because she learned a constructive way to cope.

Life is never quite the same after a severe emotional trauma, but it does go on. We cannot wait for the hurt to go away before we begin to meet life again. We cannot waste emotional energy on wishing things were different. Coping can begin only when we face the situation for what it is: There is a problem which we cannot solve to our complete satisfaction; yet life does go on, and for those willing to make the effort, it can be infinitely worth living.

7

Eight Do's and Don'ts for the Post-Crisis Period

1. Do show optimism for the future.

You don't have to show optimism for Johnny's future, although we hope that in time you will be able to. You must, however, show optimism for your home, the siblings who remain and the family's future. Dr. Martin Symonds, a psychiatrist specializing in adolescent behavior, says this concerning optimism:

> Parents have to be optimists. They have to have faith in the world and its future, or they can't expect their children to have it. Without faith, it's like an Army captain muttering, "We'll never take that hill," before the battle begins. If you really feel that the world is in a hopeless mess, hide it. Whatever you say should be honest, but don't confuse honesty with total confession; you don't have to say everything. Don't share your uncertainties about the future with your adolescent. Allow him to explore the future on his own, with your support.[1]

Perhaps at no time do adolescents need the optimism of the parent more than when an older sibling has plunged the family into chaos. And as Dr. Symonds pointed out, it should be an honest optimism without pretenses but also without total confession. It's much better to keep your personal fears concerning Johnny's future to yourself.

2. Do "double" efforts to rebuild a normal life for the rest of the family.

If siblings convey a need to discuss Johnny's problem, discuss it; but take care to get the discussion off dead center as soon as possible. Let the home life revolve around something else. Plan a weekend trip for the family. Make plans for a summer vacation. Spend an evening playing some family games.

Mother, bake someone's favorite dessert each day. Even if there is little interest in food, the family will take the cue from you and enter into the effort to regain a degree of normality. Father, how long since you have taken the family for a treat at the local ice-cream parlor or root beer stand? Don't wait for an urge; at this stage the only urge will be to quit. Think of something the family would enjoy under normal circumstances, then do it.

Have you been neglecting the world of your other children? Do you know what is going on at their school these days? Is art, music or sports important to them? Show an interest in what they are doing. They must know you care about what interests them.

Johnny's problem will be with you for a long time, but at least with concentrated effort you can force it to the side. The life of the home need no longer revolve around it.

3. Do communicate your love for Johnny to his siblings.

The children left at home need assurance that the parents still love Johnny. It is characteristic of the adolescent to react negatively to whatever the parent says or does. He easily misinterprets parental words and actions. He sees implications which are not intended. In the post-crisis period, siblings will be going through a confusion uniquely their own. Initially, they may be very critical of what Johnny has done—but they may quickly become defensive if the parent appears to communicate a lack of love for Johnny.

No doubt this sibling feels personally threatened when he senses that "Johnny has done something wrong so now my parents do not love him." Certainly he will sense his own capacity to do "something wrong" and thus jeopardize parental love for himself. Defending Johnny will, to a certain extent, constitute self-defense. You can see why parents should not judge Johnny to other children in the home. Siblings feel pulled in between, even when parents are not consciously critical of the rebelling child. Once the actual crisis is over, they are apt to feel a sibling sense of loyalty leading them to defend Johnny.

In some cases, one of the siblings yet at home may develop a sympathetic relationship with Johnny which will lead to further division in the family. This can bring about a series of problems. "Should I allow this child to visit Johnny? Should I discourage the relationship?"

To actively and vocally discourage the relationship will probably accomplish the exact opposite, so the parent in this situation is wise to move cautiously. As to visits, it will, of course, depend on several facts. How old is the sibling? What kind of trouble is Johnny involved in? Certainly a minor should not be allowed to visit Johnny if he is involved in drugs or other activities with legal implications. If, on the other hand, the remaining sibling is approaching adulthood, and if Johnny's problem does not have legal implications, the parent may find it wise to allow a visit. Some older adolescents make very objective decisions about what they see if they are not feeling pressured to take sides.

4. Don't feel you have to explain or apologize for Johnny's actions to friends and relatives.

The social contacts of the entire family may suffer some long-range effects from Johnny's actions. Some friends of long standing will communicate their feeling that you are to blame for Johnny's problems. You may find it desirable to cool certain relationships because friends cannot handle your situation. Parents do not need to continue relationships which pressure them to explain or apologize for what their adult children do.

In an extended family, you may have to handle unpleasant situations differently. For out-of-town close relatives there may come a time when you must tell most of the details. You should not feel pressured to do this until the immediate crisis is over. Then choose a time when you can either write or telephone in privacy and give the essential facts which you feel the family should know. This is your decision. For those who have praying relatives, it gives comfort to know that someone is joining with you in interceding for Johnny and upholding you and your mate as well.

5. Do be realistic about personal consequences of Johnny's actions.

While the thrust of this book may absolve parents from blame, in no way do I imply that a lack of guilt guarantees a lack of consequences. Parents cannot escape the continuing effects brought about by Johnny's rebellion. For every family with a rebelling offspring, there will be a set of consequences which must be borne corporately. It is impossible for the family to escape these consequences. Important as it is for parents to see that they are not necessarily failures because of Johnny's course of action, it is just as important that parents face the tangible problems brought about by that action.

At times, parents may find it wise to relocate. Roots may be deep, but moving may become necessary. Is that fair? Perhaps not, but seldom is life fair. In some cases, an offspring's actions actually may jeopardize a parent's job. These are big decisions and should be made with proper consideration, counsel and prayer.

6. Do face the financial crisis wisely.

Serious financial problems often result from a crisis with an offspring. The problems can become complicated when siblings at home are looking to college or have other needs. Again, big decisions may be involved.

Once Johnny has broken away, the parent should first ask himself, "Can we afford to help him?" If it would present a financial problem, then, except in the most extenuating circumstances, the parent should offer no assistance whatever. If, on the other hand, the parent can help Johnny easily, the question then becomes, "Is it good for Johnny to have our help at this point in his life? Will parental assistance diminish the chance of his living with his own decisions?" So long as Johnny has the best of two worlds he will find it difficult (and unnecessary) to be objective about the implications of his decisions.

There are times when a genuine need is there (health, transportation for work, etc.) and the parent is able, to some extent, to meet that need. The ideal, I believe, is to do so with stipulations. An informal contract calling for terms of repayment or some possession held as collateral, for example, will help Johnny see that he has now entered the adult world of business where no one gets anything for nothing.

Unfortunately some rather ugly facts of life may present themselves in the financial category. Many parents have had to face the unpleasant fact that an offspring involved in drugs soon loses all scruples in his effort to support his lifestyle. Needs quickly overcome former values until he will take anything of value from his own home to turn into ready cash. Facing reality in this case includes taking every possible measure to prevent Johnny's entering the home when no one is there.

I recall that, in one place we lived, the parents of a girl who had become involved in drugs came to us with a unique problem. They had given an heirloom ring of considerable value to their daughter. By rights the ring was hers, but the parents felt that, in a larger sense, it belonged to the family and that all measures should be taken to preserve it.

Fearing the daughter would sell the ring for drug money, they requested that we keep it in our safe. This we did for some time. As the parents had feared, a time came when the daughter demanded the ring, but they assured her it was in safekeeping for the future. The story has a happy ending for this girl later left the drug scene, went back to college and became a successful journalist. The ring has long since been returned to her and she treasures it as highly as did her parents.

7. Take care of your health.

Many parents of rebelling teens are in the prime

age bracket for stress illnesses. They also age rapidly when forced to go through several years of trying to solve all the problems heaped upon them through the rebellion. If you need proof of this statement, just compare before and after photographs of parents in this group.

One father was accused of giving a ten-year-old photo to a newspaper which was recognizing one of his recent achievements. Friends saw the picture and teased him about trying to appear younger. His best friend was aware of some of the problems this father had recently encountered, but it surprised even him to discover the picture was only two years old. The problems the father had been through had produced those aging worry lines.

The parent must concentrate on breaking stress patterns induced by the offspring's behavior. Certainly the annual physical, or semiannual one, becomes of primary importance. The parent must do everything possible to establish a positive mental outlook. I have heard parents testify that with God's help they were able to establish this, even when they didn't know the exact whereabouts of their son for months at a time.

8. Do seek a sympathetic listener.

Beware of those listeners who, even while expressing sympathy, are all too eager to point out your errors. They say, "You should have done this." "I wouldn't put up with that." "Why don't you make Johnny do this?"

Some of this well-meant but ill-timed advice will be forced upon you, but you should avoid soliciting it. It can only complicate the picture and certainly will not increase your ability to cope.

At this stage it is good for the parents to communicate with others who have known the same trials. Perhaps the parent will even feel the need to seek counsel to sort out his feelings. Such counsel must be sought with care. One father sought the counsel of an older professional and shared some of the burdens he was facing with his children. Unbelievably, he came away with nothing but the counselor's account of his own highly successful adult children. Such incidents are rare, but I cannot tell you to seek counsel and guarantee that the first counsel you receive will be helpful. You may come away, as did this father, more discouraged than ever.

Unfortunately, this is part of life also. You must sift through advice which is handed out unthinkingly, without feeling or proper understanding, and some of it may be worthless, but don't give up. Keep trying. One day just the right person will say, "Do you need a couple of waterproof shoulder pads? Come on over."

One mother had problems with several of her children. She related how she and her husband once faced a crisis, and they approached a trusted older friend. He told them, "I don't know what I can do, but I can listen." And he did. Today that mother is doing the same for others. She doesn't claim to have answers but she is a good sympathetic listener. She also is saturated in the Word of God which is her chief source of encouragement.

We began this chapter by saying that a parent should be optimistic for the sake of siblings. I close by submitting that the parent should be optimistic for himself also. Many times offspring who put parents through years of pain get through those turbulent years and then do a turnabout. As Christian parents, we must cling to the promise that the training we have given them as children will in the end be the training to which they will return. Hope for the future is something we must never lose sight of as we pray daily for those children who stray.

PART FIVE

The Parents' Right to Life

8

Is There
Life After Johnny?

After the immediate crisis is past, after long-range adjustments have been made, after new relationships are spelled out, there remains yet one more problem for Johnny's parents: "Where do we go from here?"

How do parents face the future? Can emotions so traumatized by the crisis ever heal? How can parents put their own lives back together again? Many parents feel defeated at this point because they fail to deal with that last nagging question—Can there be life after Johnny?

Right or wrong, many parents build all of life's plans around their children from the moment of conception. Those parents invest as much as a quarter of a century in the lives of their children. If Johnny manages to spare his parents the pain of rebellion, if he manages to respond to their investment in a manner which pleases them, upon his departure there is only a small matter of empty rooms to deal with. If, on the other hand, after those 25 or so years, the parents have little or no relationship left with Johnny because of problems of rebellion, there is a large matter of empty lives do deal with.

Any latent creativity about the future, the fifties or the retirement years may have remained undeveloped because the parents assumed Johnny would always be around to brighten their lives. Now that he is no longer there, the parents must call upon some resources which have lain quite dormant for several years. They must begin thinking about a future which possibly does not include Johnny.

His parents must now lay aside their dreams of extended family relationships, vacations with grandchildren, reunions, and all the other activities that would give continuous enjoyment of offspring. With all illusions gone, parents must now find new ways to make life worth living. The parents' primary goal must now be to reconstruct their own personal lives.

The parent must decide for life

The parent who discovers life after Johnny must act decisively. His first step is to choose life over mere existence. The parent must recognize there is a difference between coping and living. As essential as it is to learn to cope, this must never become an end in itself. Coping is not the same as living.

Unfortunately, many times when the crisis has passed, the parent who has learned to cope assumes he has done all that can be done. He mistakes the ability to ward off hurt for the ability to find solutions. Some build walls to avoid further pain, and they become so used to the walls that they are unaware of their presence. This is a withdrawal process, and it happens to a lot of people. Parents of estranged children are particularly vulnerable to emotional withdrawal.

In the course of my husband's ministry he often does a personality profile analysis for those he counsels. He has found this to be an extremely valuable tool. Its purpose is to picture how the individual views himself and to reveal possible problems. One of the problems it pinpoints is that of withdrawal.

Recently, he had an interesting experience with this process. A father was retaking a test after a span of four years. This man, normally outgoing and sociable, had gradually become quieter, keeping to himself for the most part. Since his work demands constant contact with people, there were those who had noticed the change. The man himself was completely oblivious to it. The results of the test surprised him when they showed how withdrawn he had become since the previous testing.

In reviewing the events of his life in the last four years, he and my husband discovered that his first analysis had been done just one month before the onset of a crisis with his teenage son. During that period, the crisis had somewhat resolved itself and the father had learned to cope successfully with a number of unpleasant situations, but that was as far as he went.

In dealing with his own hurt, he had subconsciously cut himself off from all but the most rudimentary social contact. He went through the motions on his job, but he actually had lost interest in people and in life. He was existing. In this man's case, once he saw the pattern he had created, he began to break it, through concentrated effort. It demanded decisive action on his part. His success was due largely to his dissatisfaction with mere existence. He chose life.

The parent must assume control of his own situation

A parent can assume control of his own situation even if he cannot control Johnny. In fact, when a parent assumes control of his own situation it has nothing to do with what Johnny does or does not do. It has to do with the parent's reactions, his own outlook and his personal plans. It has to do with assuming control of self, not of offspring or of circumstances.

When our children were quite small we had a beautiful water spaniel puppy. For reasons long forgotten we neglected to have the necessary shots for him and when he was about eight months old he contracted distemper. For days the girls kept vigil over that sick little dog. Our middle daughter still remembers how "unfeeling" her father was when he found her kneeling beside the dog with a dish towel half in the dog's bed and half on the floor. The sight of it provoked some rather stern words from Father. Our daughter felt it was completely inhuman to scold her simply because she could not concentrate on such mundane chores as drying dishes when Rags was so critically ill. When the dog died, the girls cried for two days and no amount of comfort would stem their tears.

On the third morning, our youngest, then six, marched into the living room and announced, "Well, I've had enough. I'm not going to cry any more!"

And that was that. She could not change the circumstances, but in her childish wisdom she took charge of her own situation when she decided not to cry any more.

Taking charge of one's situation is an individual matter. Our daughter did not wait for her older sisters to make the first move or even to agree with her. Ideally, both parents will come to the place where they will opt for living over mere existing, but to wait for one's spouse may defeat the one trying to assume control of his own situation. Someone must make the first move, whether or not the spouse falls into step.

Follow decision with action

My husband's secretary once tacked a cartoon up on the office door. It was a picture of five frogs sitting on a log. The caption asked the question, "If there were five frogs on a log and one decided to jump, how many would still be on the log?" A fold in the cartoon formed a pocket from which the curious could draw a card containing the answer. It read, "Five would still be there. Deciding to jump is not the same as jumping."

The parent who is truly decisive will follow decision with action.

Finding life after Johnny is a self-help program which demands determination over feelings, and action over inertia. It calls for a schedule which allows for development of the physical, mental and social areas of life. The parent doesn't have to launch a full-scale self-improvement program, but he should take inventory of the neglected areas of his life and take immediate steps to correct the situation.

Consider first the **physical.** In addition to health, discussed in chapter 7, the physical area of life involves such things as exercise and personal grooming. What type of exercise have you enjoyed in the past? Have you been keeping it up during the period of Johnny's rebellion? Has the tennis racquet been confined to the closet? Is the fishing pole gathering dust? Have you forgotten where you put your bowling ball? Now is the time to drag out those things and put them to use.

Perhaps you have always wanted to learn a certain sport. Now is the time to add this to your schedule. Recently my husband became interested in sailing. One reason he enjoys it so much is that he finds he must give it his complete attention. It is a total diversion from work and problems. Be realistic about your ability and your physical fitness, and choose something at which you can expect a degree of success. You don't need one more thing in your life to undermine your self-confidence. And of course we must undertake any exercise program wisely.

Our personal physician has advised us consistently against jogging because he believes that strenuous exercise should either be done regularly or not at all. For us the doctor's advice has continually been, "Take a brisk two-mile walk every day."

A good evaluation of **personal grooming** may be in order at this point. In the face of emotional trauma over which the parent has no control, he can easily lose interest in lesser matters over which he could exercise control. When we lose interest in life, we sometimes lose interest in our personal appearance. Examine this carefully. Determine to give a certain amount of time each day to personal appearance. Include such things as manicures, pedicures, skin treatment, hair care and all those extra areas which may need attention.

How about your **wardrobe**? Have you let it go just because you were in such a zombie state you could not decide what to buy? Have you ignored it because you didn't care about such trivial things in light of the greater problem?

In addition to the physical, take inventory of the **mental** area of your life. Stretching the mind seems to be necessary for people who have reached a plateau in their lives and are floundering, not knowing what to do next. Have you considered taking classes at the local college? Although I am not particularly creative, I have noticed that for those who are, there are many opportunities today. Most local colleges offer classes designed to encourage adults to develop their creative skills.

For the more academic, there are correspondence courses. I discovered that the local extension service from one of our state universities offers a correspondence course in German. Learning that language had interested me, and I have some personal background with it, so I enrolled. In my experience, I have found few things which occupy the mind more completely than the study of a foreign language.

Certainly you need not limit yourself to local colleges or correspondence courses. Set up your own reading program in a subject you wish to study. Attend some lectures. The opportunities are there for the parent who decides to stretch his mind a bit.

Finally, let us consider the area of **social** contact. The social area of life is extremely important for that parent who is electing for new life after Johnny. It is not something which will come automatically. The parent must determine to get out and make contacts. Don't wait for the mood to hit. Many people can very easily bury themselves in work, problems and projects and never be aware of missing social contact.

Sometimes I do this myself, and in the process I become rather introverted. Usually, when I break the routine and get out it is not because I suddenly decide, "Hey, I want to get out of this house and see someone"; or, "Wait, honey, I'll pack a bag and go with you this trip." It is more apt to be because I force myself to break the pattern, and get out and communicate with someone. Just visiting an old friend or going somewhere different is enough. Whenever I return from the experience of communicating with some other human in any small way, I am again a different person. More responsive. Happier. More content. More objective about my problems. The point? If you wait to resume social contact until you feel the need, you will never change the pattern. In reconstructing a life, I am convinced that actions come first and feeling follows.

We cannot assume you will need the same amount or the same type of social contact as any other parent. Neither can we assume you will have the same needs after your traumatic experience that you had before it. It may be that through your experience you have had to drop contact with some casual acquaintances. People are sometimes insensitive. Friends may need you to fulfill their needs but show little compassion or concern for yours.

It is difficult to maintain much social contact with those who either have not understood your problem or who have not been able to handle it. Still you need some social contact. The circle may be smaller, more intimate, made up primarily of new friends met in the post-Johnny period. Build your own circle and cultivate friendships carefully.

Another form of social contact is social action. This is a constructive way to deal with your own needs while also meeting another's. So many worthy organizations need volunteers—your political party, the local hospital, your church—all of these agencies are in constant need of people willing to get involved.

Perhaps you learned something through your experience that has awakened an interest in a certain area. In the beginning, a parent may wish to get as far away as possible from anything that reminds him of the problem. After time has done its work, though, many parents feel differently. They want to get involved in preventing some of the things which caused them such heartache.

Recently a mother who faced problems with all three of her children remarked that she would like to work in some capacity with troubled teens. At this point she doesn't know how or where, but with determination she is preparing herself for opportunities that may come.

There are no set rules for developing the physical, mental or social areas of life. Each parent has different needs, different likes and dislikes. The important thing is to get active in pursuing those things which are a personal challenge. At this point in life, if the parent is to find healing for his damaged emotions, if he is to reconstruct a meaningful life, he must consider his own personal needs.

The parent who continues to consider Johnny's needs to the exclusion of his own will impede the **emotional** healing process. There must come a point where the parent acknowledges, "Johnny has made his choice. I can no longer concentrate all my efforts toward preventing him from destroying himself. I must now see that I am not destroyed in the aftermath."

Emotional healing can never depend on a change in Johnny. That may never happen. The parent must not wait for Johnny to change before he begins to reconstruct his own life.

Reconstructing the life also will involve reconstructing the marriage and for some, reconstructing one's spiritual life. We will deal with these subjects in the next two chapters.

If every parent had a success story, this would not be necessary. However, as long as the propagation of the human race continues, some parents will face disappointment and depression brought on by the actions of their offspring. If you are one of these parents, and through this book you discover there can be life after Johnny, the book will have accomplished its goal.

PARENTAL PROJECT

Assuming Control of Self

PROJECT: FOR THE INDIVIDUAL PARENT

I. _Think_ about these things:

- Assuming control of your life demands some positive thinking, a habit which you may have lost through the crisis with Johnny.

- Use the following exercise to get yourself started again. Timing yourself for one minute, complete question #1 with as many answers as possible.

- Repeat with question #2.

1. I think these things make life worth living:

2. I really enjoy:

II. _Ponder and complete_ these statements:

1. I would feel better about myself if:

2. I would like the way I look if only:

3. I feel good about the way I look when:

4. My wardrobe needs:

5. My skin needs attention _____yes _____no

6. My hair needs attention _____yes _____no

7. My weight needs attention _____yes _____no

8. I need a checkup _____yes _____no

9. I need to resume regular exercise

_____yes _____no

III. *Projects for getting your mind off your problems:*

1. On the basis of the above statements, compile a list of shopping needs. Decide whether statement 5, 6, 7 or 8 needs a professional appointment. Make it.

2. Squander a whole afternoon on personal grooming.

3. Read an Erma Bombeck book.

4. Take a friend to lunch.

5. Spend an afternoon at the park.

6. Investigate local opportunities for mind stretching (college classes, seminars, crafts, hobbies).

7. Learn a new skill.

8. Attend a concert.

9. Investigate needs for volunteers in your church, your community and your political party.

10. Do something nice for your spouse.

9

Can We Begin Again, Lord?

For the Christian parent, if there is to be life after Johnny, it may be necessary to begin again in a spiritual sense. We are never the same after a traumatic experience. For better or for worse, we are forever changed through those things which touch our lives. The trauma experienced through the loss of an offspring to some form of rebellion may cause a temporary regression of the spiritual life. For this parent, the most important question becomes, "Can we begin again, Lord?"

When I first met Gordon, he was making a new beginning in his spiritual life. As a Christian, he had spent years shoving aside unresolved problems. The resulting accumulation of guilt made serious inroads into his relationship with God. Then one night someone told him what to do about his guilt, real or imagined. That night Gordon started over. This is his story.

Although Gordon is a warm, loving and outgoing individual who holds a responsible position in his community, for years he saw himself only as a parent who had failed. He went through a divorce when his children were approaching adolescence. There had been problems in the marriage. In a sense, the divorce simply exchanged one set of problems for another. In the first place, as a Christian, Gordon did not really believe in divorce. Death of a marriage meant death of an ideal and ideals die hard. He felt very guilty over the marriage breakup.

In the second place, he felt extremely guilty over the effects (real or imagined) of the divorce upon his sons. Much of this guilt stemmed from one past incident which he could not forget. He remembered a day when his tenderhearted little son was moved to tears because the parents of his best friend divorced. The incident so affected the boy that Gordon took his son in his arms, comforted him and promised, "Son, you don't ever have to worry about anything like that happening to your parents. It never will." Of course, it did. The thought of that broken promise haunted Gordon for years.

Because Gordon is both intelligent and aggressive, he had no problem finding success and wealth, but he was a lonely man. There were nights, he confesses, that in his loneliness he cried throughout the night for his boys. Inevitably he slipped into the pattern of trying to buy their love. Elaborate vacations were standard procedure for the times they spent with him. To illustrate the extremity of his problem, Gordon tells how he spent enormous amounts of money decorating his bachelor apartment, buying sterling silverware, table linens, etc., for a holiday visit from his sons. He wanted everything to be perfect for the little time they would be together.

Such unwise parental actions generated a predictable response from two growing boys. First his sons used him, and second, in time they actually rejected him.

When Gordon woke up to the situation, he made a series of adjustments in his dealings with them. Eventually, he developed a good relationship with his sons, but he still carried his load of guilt.

Meanwhile, he remarried and his life began to take on a new dimension. Loneliness no longer plagued him, but he felt responsible for every problem the boys faced in their teenage years. Every time he heard that one of the boys was in trouble, he blamed himself. "I wasn't there when they needed me," he explains.

The boys were grown before Gordon faced the regression in his own spiritual life due to the unresolved guilt. It happened one night at a seminar sponsored by Campus Crusade. The speaker instructed those attending to write down on paper all their mistakes and sins of the past that they could think of. Then the leader asked them to pray and confess those sins to God. Finally he instructed them to write across the list: *Forgiven.*

"It was a new beginning," Gordon declares. "God took care of all of my confusion and guilt." That beginning was the basis for reconstruction of his spiritual life.

1. Wiping the slate clean

For those who would make a new beginning spiritually, the first step is to wipe the slate clean. That means dealing with mistakes. Certainly we as parents do make mistakes, but as one mother observed, "I did the best I could with the knowledge I had at the time. I've asked the Lord to forgive my mistakes and I know He has." First John 1:9 must become a reality in the life of the parent who needs a new spiritual beginning:

> If we confess our sins, he is faithful and just to forgive us our sins, and to cleanse us from all unrighteousness.

Gordon found forgiveness on this basis, not because someone said, "Stop feeling guilty."

Wiping the slate clean also means dealing with bitterness. There can be no spiritual renewal as long as a parent feels bitter over what has happened. A parent is vulnerable to bitterness. Many parents are idealists, and no one is as positive as an idealist whose values have never been tested. When those ideals have been through the crucible, though, the idealist will emerge either a stronger person or a bitter, disillusioned person. You do not remain the same after your theories about the most important things in life are put to the test.

Job's strengthening

The testing of ideals should serve to deepen the Christian's relationship with God. Consider Job. Satan thought him an untested idealist. In fact, Satan told God that anyone can be strong if he has God's hedge around him. So God allowed Job to be put through the crucible.

He lost everything, his friends became accusers, and even his wife said, "Curse God and die." Then Job, after careful self-examination, discerned that it was a time of testing, and his relationship with God deepened. Job's ideals were confronted—and he came out stronger.

"Though he slay me," Job said in 13:15, "yet will I trust in him." What could have been a bitter experience became a maturing experience. Out of his suffering came the theme which still expresses the hope of every believer, "I know that my Redeemer liveth!" (19:25).

David's strengthening

Consider also David. He is an even greater example for the parent who suffers because of rebelling children. His son, Absalom, rose up against his own father. It was a dark time for David. He lost the loyalty of his closest friends. His chief counsel defected to Absalom. A troublemaker erroneously reported that Mephibosheth, grandson of Saul, had seized the opportunity and staked his claim to the throne. Shimei followed David, cursing, spitting, throwing stones and showering the king with dirt. Bitterness could be expected. David had selflessly served the very people who then hunted him down, but the crucible—even the trauma of Absalom's rebellion—served to bring David closer to God.

Bitterness is like a cancerous growth. It soon dominates the life it invades. It accomplishes only one thing, the destruction of the life over which it gains control.

If Johnny's actions have left you bitter, wipe the slate clean. Confess this bitterness to God. That means calling it exactly what God calls it. It means praying a simple prayer, "Lord, I confess I am bitter. Forgive me."

2. Understanding the value of suffering

Second Corinthians 1:3,4 describes the God of all comfort by saying that He "comforts us in all our troubles, so that we can comfort those in any trouble with the comfort we ourselves have received from God" (NIV).

Jennifer recently remarked how she is discovering this truth. Since her children are not yet in school, she knows little of the parental suffering we have been discussing. However, about a year ago she and her husband went through an extremely difficult period. At the time, neither knew how they would survive. Today she states that they learned some lessons they never would have learned apart from the suffering they endured. The most exciting thing to Jennifer now is that she has met a young woman her age who is experiencing the same difficulty, and Jennifer has been able to encourage her.

"I couldn't believe it," Jennifer said, "but I could encourage her just by assuring her that we have been down that road ourselves." She is learning that suffering is valuable because it enables us to sympathize with others who have the same problems.

Rarely does comfort come from those who have not known suffering. Experience seems to precede empathy. Ruth Bell Graham expresses this thought:

> They felt good eyes upon them
> and shrank within — undone;
> good parents had good children
> and they — a wandering one.
> The good folk never meant
> to act smug or condemn,
> but having prodigals
> just "wasn't done" with them.
> Remind them gently, Lord,
> how You
> have trouble with Your children
> too.[1]

The value of suffering as a teacher and a refiner has been expressed by many poets, theologians and songwriters. One of my favorites is Audrey Mieir's beautiful song, "Don't Spare Me."

> Forgive me Lord, I've prayed in vain
> That You would spare me grief and pain,
> But now my blinded eyes can see
> These things were best for me.
>
> Don't spare me trouble if it will bring me close to Thee.
> Don't spare me heartaches; You bore a broken heart for me.
> Don't spare me loneliness, for I recall Gethsemane.
> Don't spare me anything that You endured for me.
> Don't spare me failure if this is what is best for me.
> Don't spare me sickness if this will make me call on Thee.
> Don't spare me suffering, for I recall Your agony.
> Don't spare me anything that You endured for me;
> but give me strength to follow Thee.[2]

3. Making a new commitment to God

To begin again, we must commit ourselves to **study** His Word, to **pray** and to **be available to comfort others** who also suffer. The personal Bible study program of the parent becomes essential to progress at this point. My good friend Lillian explains a time of deep trouble by saying, "I was groveling my way through the psalms." The psalms can bring much comfort, even in those times when we are at our lowest.

Studying the Word

Beyond the comfort there must also come a deeper look at the Word and it must be done on a systematic, daily basis. Begin by setting aside a good time – the earlier in your day, the better. Try a book study, or do a character study. Have you ever read the life of Moses or David, looking at their attitudes and reactions to problems? This makes an enlightening study.

Whatever you choose to study, do try to look beyond the actions recorded and find the attitudes. Write down your observations. Especially note any which seem to parallel your own attitudes at this stage of your life. On a separate page you may want to list any spiritual lessons learned through your experience with Johnny. Also note any negative attitudes which the experience has caused to surface. Through your study, you soon will begin to see how attitudes affected the outcome of many situations recorded in the Scripture. Personal applications will become obvious. The Word of God can help you grow as a result of your experience.

Praying

Add a new dimension to your prayer life. In addition to praying for Johnny and his continuing problem, pray, "Lord, make me a blessing to someone today. And

Lord, teach me through Thy Word." Make a prayer list. Pray for other parents who suffer. Keep a prayer diary or a file.

Many years ago while attending Biola College, I received a prayer file from a friend. A simple recipe size file box, it contained cards indexed for each day of the week plus one section marked "Answered." Through the years it has served as an aid to prayer. When our children were small and demanded my constant attention, many times I would prop the cards up above the sink or on the ironing board because time was so short. Parents whose children have grown are more free to arrange a daily meeting with God over a prayer list. Make this a part of your recommitment program.

Comforting others

As you study and pray, you will prepare yourself for that third part of your recommitment program, comforting others by the same comfort you have received in your suffering. Remember, it is enough to say, "I know what you are going through." You don't have to repeat all your trials. That is no comfort unless you are citing some point at which the Lord gave special comfort.

What the other person needs most is a good listener. Sharing a verse or a passage of Scripture is also important if it has been important to you. Preaching a sermon, on the other hand, is not helpful. Praying *with* the one who suffers as well as *for* him is a comfort.

No matter what the trauma in life, the spiritually oriented person will not be the same in its wake. Suffering because of children is just the same as any other suffering insofar as the spiritual lesson learned is concerned. Eventually, every individual must face that incident in life which reduces him to the knowledge that no human help is available. Such times as these teach us a more complete trust in God's dealing with our lives.

Such times also prompt a reassessment of spiritual goals. Emerging from the other side of the traumatic experience, the parent may see that some of his worthy goals were slightly off-course. For example, a mother may have been challenged by the scriptural example of Hannah who prayed for a son and then presented that son to the Lord. Hannah's story may have inspired the mother to raise her children in such a way as to be pleasing to the Lord. Her spiritual goal becomes the same as Hannah's. She wants to offer her child in some way to the Lord, so she spends her life trying to mold and shape the life of her child. Her daily prayer is, "Lord, You gave me this wonderful gift, this dear little life. In appreciation for this life You have lent me, I am molding and shaping it as You would desire."

Then one day the child grows up and exercises his God-given will in quite the opposite direction of his parents' wishes — and the mother finds herself in a lonely and desolate place. Quite empty-handed, she stands with nothing to offer the Lord.

Well, not quite empty-handed. She has herself. Perhaps that is what the Lord wanted in the first place. It is at this point of desolation that the mother must reassess her spiritual goals. She now offers a revised version of that daily prayer, "Lord, I have nothing left to offer You, except myself — but I gladly offer You that."

Can we begin again, Lord?

PARENTAL PROJECT

Spiritual Recommitment

1. If you haven't already done so, set aside a special time for daily Bible study.

2. Make a list of the spiritual lessons you have learned through your experience.

3. Make a list of other parents who are going through similar experiences. Pray daily for them.

4. Count your blessings.

5. Set aside a regular time for prayer.

6. Make a list of parents with success stories. Thank God for the way He has worked in the lives of those sons or daughters and pray for their continued obedience to Him.

7. Attend a retreat.

8. Visit someone who is lonely.

9. Visit a Christian bookstore. Buy a new book. Read it!

10. Count your blessings again.

* * * * *

For more information on how to have the joy and power of the Holy Spirit in your life, see the appendix, "Have You Made the Wonderful Discovery?" beginning on page 154.

10

We
Still Have
Each Other

When Johnny is the last child to leave home, the parents are left with an additional problem.

For weeks, months, and sometimes years, they have concentrated all their efforts on finding a solution for Johnny's problem. They've had little time to think of anything else. Now they face the inevitable—Johnny is gone and there is nothing more they can do. There are no other tailspinning siblings in the home, either, to demand their parental love and attention. These parents face an immediate void. For better or for worse, they are back to square one.

They are alone . . . but they still have each other. Or do they?

"The teenage years present a real test to the solidity of the marriage," my friend Peggy, a high school counselor, observed astutely. We had been discussing some of the problems of adolescents when she shifted the focus to the problems of their parents.

Of course, anything which puts a strain on the home will likely put a strain on the marriage, and vice versa. I think there are only three things about which couples fight: sex, money and the children (make that four if there are in-law problems). Which stage of life they are in will determine which item occupies top place on the list. As children reach the teenage years, parents find themselves quarreling more about their offspring.

When a family has been through a teenage rebellion crisis culminating in Johnny's leaving home, a reassessment of the marriage may need to take place. If the marriage is in trouble, the situation back at square one becomes, "We still have each other if we work at it."

I do not believe good marriages result by accident or by Cupid's irresistible bow and arrow. Show me a happy couple and I will show you two people who work at their marriage. Throughout a marriage, critical periods will arise where this is especially true. The post-Johnny era is one of them. Parents who seek to find life after Johnny must recognize the need to work at their marriage. Certainly the post-crisis reconstruction process will be completed more quickly and easily if trouble in the marriage is at a minimum.

Put the past behind

Earlier we spoke of the need to wipe the slate clean if we want to begin again spiritually. This is also true when it comes to the marriage. In the post-Johnny period, working at marriage is like beginning again. The first step is to determine to put the past behind. There are two basic negative principles to follow when putting the past behind: (1) Don't blame each other; and (2) don't look back.

To blame the other person for Johnny's problem

may be a temptation, but rarely can any family disaster be laid at the feet of one parent. In such cases where it may be justified, there must come forgiveness and a frank acknowledgement that you are mates in all of life for better or for worse. So be generous with your spouse. There is nothing so useless as the admonition, "You should have done it this way," when there will never again be the opportunity to do it *any* way.

It is so important that you and your spouse lay aside the past and determine not to look back. We must make decisions every day of our lives. Human error is a necessary risk of daily living. How tormented we become, how unsure of ourselves, how incompetent, if we continually examine those decisions and wonder, "Did I do right?"

This is especially true concerning parental responsibilities. No other job compares to parenthood — by the time we learn how to do the job it is too late. Accept the fact that a stage of your life is over. If you can't look back remembering the laughter, don't look back.

Renew your courtship

Once parents deal with the past, they should apply themselves to today and tomorrow, and all the tomorrows they have together. Reconstructing the marriage is, to some extent, like renewing a courtship. You begin again. Only now you are older, wiser, perhaps less starry-eyed. You are beginning from a different perspective. Still you begin in much the same way.

What pleases your mate? What are the things you can do for your other half? Think about your courtship period. You wanted to do things to please that person who was always in your thoughts. Cooking a man's favorite dishes, achieving the look he appreciates, and saying things he likes to hear, are all part of a woman's daily routine during the courting period. The man, in turn, often surprises the object of his affections with inexpensive little gifts, an impromptu outing, compliments and tender words. Favorite dishes may now be low calorie, compliments may take a different form, and outings may necessarily be less strenuous, but the basic principle is just the same.

In his book, *Men in Mid-Life Crisis,* Jim Conway conveys optimism concerning parents left alone after the children are gone:

> Children also influence marital happiness. In the early years of marriage, children tend to build an emotional bond between a man and his wife. During their adolescent years, children tend to drive down their parents' emotional happiness. After the couple has passed the empty nest and mid-life crisis, marital happiness improves with the absence of children allowing the couple to relate to each other more intimately. [1]

The goal of parents in the post-Johnny era should be to relate to one another more intimately.

Encourage one another

In addition to courtship renewal, you should make a determined effort to encourage your mate to pursue that which is important to him (her). Can you encourage your mate to do something simply because you know he has always wanted to do it? Should he start a new hobby? Resume a neglected one? Pursue a degree? Develop a talent? Whatever you do to encourage your mate will benefit both of you, now and in the future.

Set new goals

Even if you are not primarily goal-centered as a

couple, this is a good time to set a few. It gives new purpose to life. Make your goals in two categories: "Let's
share today," and, "Let's plan for the future."

When our nest became empty, my husband and I
set two goals. First, we made the daily walk—that we always had intended to get around to—a part of our routine. Each day at six A.M. we took a two-and-a-half-mile
walk. That was our "Let's share today" goal.

We also began to plan together for a future hike
into Havasupai village. For you nonwesterners, I should
explain that this last vestige of paradise with its famous
Supai Falls, is located on the floor of the Grand Canyon.
I had dreamed of going to this village for years. My husband was less enthusiastic ("If you want to go with your
first husband, Joy, you'd better hurry up!"), but he was
willing to pursue the goal with me.

It took a few years, but eventually we reached our
goal. One September we managed to keep up with a
dozen single young adults on a backpacking trip to Havasupai. It was strenuous, but it was an unforgettable experience.

It all began because, when our last daughter left
home, the house was too quiet, too big, and too empty.
My husband and I knew that if we were to survive our
empty nest period we would have to find some new ways
to share each day.

Whether or not you take a daily walk together,
you should set aside some portion of the day to do something together. Sitting across the table from one another
does not count. Years ago a frustrated mother of two toddlers related to me that her doctor told her, "You and
your husband have to find something you can do together
every day, if it's nothing more than going out in the yard

and pulling a weed or two." What is necessary for younger parents is just as essential for parents in a post-Johnny period.

Vary the routine

Not only should you set goals which lead to more time being spent together, but you should also seek to vary your routine. Routines developed out of necessity can become very dull over the years. Does your husband like to sneak out late at night to the Dairy Queen, the Pizza Hut, or to the Dunkin' Donut shop? For years you couldn't leave little Johnny home alone. Then came the adolescent period, and any time the urge for a late night foray hit hubby, Johnny had the car.

Now there is no excuse. Perhaps your wife has always wanted to eat out more but your responsibilities as a provider for a growing family made it economically impossible. This is a good time to revise the budget to include an occasional night out for the cook. There is no better period in life for varying the routine than right now.

Compromise creatively

During the post-Johnny period, parents will be able to spend prime time together if they learn to make use of creative compromise. The day our daughter left, I cried. All day. I cleaned her room, packed away the few things left behind and talked to her poodle, who spent the day sniffing out every corner of her room. The next day I packed my suitcase and went with my husband to a three-day conference.

I had the usual excuses for staying home: I didn't have time to go. I had deadlines to meet. I couldn't spare three more days in addition to my time off for crying.

My husband had two reasons I should go: I needed

to get away. He wanted me with him.

So we compromised. I packed a briefcase, my manuscript file and my typewriter. I worked at the motel during the day while he attended the meetings. Together we had dinner each evening, attended the evening sessions and went out for late night snacks with friends.

We both accomplished what we set out to accomplish, and we spent some prime time together in the process. In fact, it worked so well we have repeated the arrangement several times since. With only two schedules to consider, a couple can do much more together if they are willing to compromise a little.

Seek stimulation

As you and your mate work through this time of adjustment, you need to concentrate on finding situations and people who stimulate you. Whether through a new challenge or by making some new friends, aggressively seek the stimulations which add zest to life.

Begin to set goals for the future. What is it you have always wanted to do but never dared? Now is the time to investigate every possibility. Some ideas may have to be discarded. Let's face it, we can't all climb Mount Everest or become a world champion golfer, but other things may be within the realm of possibility. Possible goals may include a new home, remodeling the one you have, taking some night classes together, or traveling.

Have you dreamed of going to Europe? Investigating the options may show you it would be easier than you thought. There are many ways to cut costs if you are willing to put the time and effort into planning your own trip abroad. For example, airfares are much more affordable if you buy tickets well in advance, take advantage of off-season rates, or go with a charter group. Even for those who do not have to budget that stringently, a do-it-yourself plan is still a great way to go because planning such a trip is half the fun.

You may not want to travel to Europe, hike to Havasupai or even go out for a midnight pizza, but it is essential that you invest the time and effort required to reconstruct your marriage after Johnny has gone. This investment will pay high dividends because the complexion of your entire future depends on it.

Do what's right for YOU

According to Jim Conway, that future could equal half of your total married life. "Because families have fewer children, parents today begin to experience the empty nest when the parents are in their forties. Yet, since life expectancy has increased dramatically—both parents may expect to live into their seventies—couples now have half of their marriage without children in the home."[2]

In families where the relationships remain good, extended family situations involving grandchildren and married sons and daughters will fill at least a part of those years. Many parents no longer consider it necessary, though, to plan their future around the extended family after the children are grown.

"Death of a Fairy Tale"[3] is the story of one young couple who wanted traditional close-by grandparents for their children but whose parents had other ideas. Both sets of parents retired the same year. One moved to California and the other to Florida. It was a shock to the young couple to find that their parents wanted to build lives for themselves in spite of their love for their children and the good relationships they maintained. In time, the couple adjusted and came to see that their parents had a right to make such choices.

Parents who lose temporary contact with their adult offspring because of problems of rebellion will feel a great void. For them, making creative choices for the future is more than a right. It is essential for survival. I do not advocate all parents relocating in Florida or California (or Arizona!), but I do advocate that parents in the post-Johnny era concentrate on what seems right for the two of them. When parents begin to ask, "What can we do for each other?" and, "What can we do together?" it does not mean they have suddenly grown selfish. It does mean they are consciously striving to strengthen their own relationship. Anything which strengthens the parents' marriage will prove beneficial to everyone concerned.

PARENTAL PROJECT

Serious and Silly Things to Do
WITH or FOR Your Spouse

PROJECT: FOR THE COUPLE

1. If you are the cook in the family, plan a special meal just for your spouse.

2. Plan an evening out for your spouse. (A date, in other words!)

3. Set aside an evening at home to talk about wild dreams for the future. (It costs nothing to dream, so always begin with the dream, and then see what can fit into the budget and the physical limitations.)

4. Encourage your spouse in some specific area today.

5. Plan a weekend away soon. (Together, that is!)

6. Buy a gift for your spouse today. (It doesn't have to be expensive, just thoughtful.)

7. Invite some friends in for dessert. (Don't talk about kids!)

8. Pick up some travel folders today and study them together.

9. Spend an evening browsing through your favorite department store looking at home furnishings, clothing or hobby items.

10. Encourage your spouse to talk about himself (herself) this evening. Ask him to tell you something "funny about yourself" or "something you've always wanted to do." (Be a good listener!)

11. Go out for a midnight snack.

12. Have you hugged your spouse today?

PART SIX

The Parents' Gift of Love

"If" for Parents

If you can love your child
through each stormy teenage year,

If you can keep your standards
when his begin to disappear,

If you can dream for your child
and watch the dream begin to crumble,

If you can reason with him
when you're tempted to berate,

If you can remember his laughter
long after he begins to grumble,

If you can pray and hope and
not go blaming fate,

If you can bear to hear the counsel you've given
twisted by a rash and angry son,
or watch him go his way until he's broken
then stoop to pick him up, no matter what he's done,

If you can wait and not be tired by waiting,

If you can separate the lying from the one who lies
and seeing the hate, love the one who does the hating
yet not seem cold, unfeeling and pompously wise,

If you can love when he no longer needs you,

If you can reach out when he seems to turn away,

If you can live with optimism too
by looking beyond the present to a future day,

If you can dream and wait and love and pray,
then you can learn to smile along the way.

What's more, you can truthfully say,
"I did my best;
now let God take care of the rest."

© 1979, by Joy P. Gage, Yuma, Arizona

11

Love Letters to Sons and Daughters

When a parent faces the myriad problems of an estranged child, he often finds himself in a position where the only thing he can offer that child is love. The parent cannot offer support for fear of condoning his child's actions. He cannot offer guidance for fear of interfering. He cannot offer financial aid for fear of underwriting a lifestyle which he abhors. He cannot even smooth over some of the rough places for the child because that would diminish the child's ability to live with his own decision.

Through this period the parent faces the rather complicated task of communicating "I love you, Johnny" without communicating "I approve of what you are doing." When the parent takes the necessary pains to express his love, he is doing the most important thing he can do for his child.

Unfortunately, communication becomes a never-ending problem. Although Johnny has demanded full freedom from parental authority, he is unsure about how that freedom is supposed to affect their relationship. He knows he doesn't want them to tell him what to do. He is relieved when he realizes they have recognized he is an adult and have discontinued their nagging. Often, though, he is not prepared to face the other changes which follow.

Telephone conversations will be guarded and letters will be rather stilted. The entire relationship will be somewhat superficial during the initial period of the estrangement. Parents can understand the cause of this but usually Johnny can't. Perhaps a sense of guilt interferes with his objectivity. Perhaps it's just that his parents are much older and have more experience and a better perspective. They realize that relinquishing the authority also means letting go of the responsibility. Some parents experience a vague sense of relief about this. A certain alleviation of pressure comes with the end of a war, even when all the battles have been lost.

Unexpectedly, Johnny may find himself bewildered by the whole process. He may begin to sense his parents' relief and he sees this as an indication that they are glad to be free of him. (He had expected it to be the other way around.) He may express his confusion by accusing his parents of not loving him, of being distant, of favoring siblings yet at home, or of discouraging a mutually intimate relationship.

Understandably, some complicated communication problems develop. Explosive conversations are only one part of the problem. If the estranged child moves to another city, a whole new set of communication problems develop. Sometimes the child will drop out of sight for months at a time. Sometimes he gives a false address, using a friend's home for a mail drop. Or Johnny may write regularly, but misinterpret every letter received from his parents.

In this chapter are some excerpts of letters written by parents to estranged children. Each of these parents was trying to assure the child, "We love you." Each also tried to do this without compromising his own values or diminishing the responsibility of the estranged child. This is no easy task.

The letters are not presented as perfect examples, nor as final solutions. They were chosen because they represent a variety of problems: A widowed mother counsels her daughter on some of the consequences of cohabitation outside of marriage. A father explains to a son in prison why no one has complete freedom to live as he chooses. A mother sympathizes with a daughter's suffering. A father deals with a son's imagined rejection. A mother reaches out to a son whose contacts are becoming fewer and farther between.

I hope that from these letters you will gain some insight into handling communication with an estranged son or daughter. The letters are, in a very real sense, love letters from parents to their adult children.

Letter #1

A widowed mother shares this correspondence with her daughter. The occasion of the letters was the fiftieth anniversary celebration for the paternal grandparents. The daughter writes:

> Mom,
>
> Today I received an invitation from Aunt Trish for the 50th wedding anniversary party for Grandma and Grandad. She enclosed a note saying how they were all counting on my being there since I am the only granddaughter, etc., etc.

Have you told them about me and Joe? I am afraid Grandma and Grandad might not understand, and I certainly don't want to be accused of ruining the whole day. If they don't already know and it came out at the party, they might be hurt. I wouldn't want everyone in the family upset with me for spoiling their party.

Could you explain that I just couldn't make it?

Judy

The mother replies:

My dear daughter,

Your letter concerning the party for your grandparents came yesterday. I have thought a lot about it, and have decided the time has come to communicate some of those things left unsaid when you made your bid for "freedom."

Three months ago when you and Joe decided to set up housekeeping, I did everything I could to prevent your doing so, but I had to accept the fact that you are 21. I have tried to live with this even though your actions go against everything I believe in and everything I stand for. So far, my decision to accept the facts has worked to your advantage. Now you will see that this will not always be the case.

To answer your two questions: No, I have not told your grandparents (or anyone else) that when you moved 300 miles away it was to move in with your boyfriend. And no, I will not make any excuses or explanations for you. I know the invitation calls for R.S.V.P. You may go or not go as you wish, but it is your responsibility to make your own excuses.

When you were little and sometimes misbehaved at your grandmother's home, it was my responsibility to correct and to control you. Sometimes it was even necessary for me to apologize for your actions, but when I relinquished the right to control your actions, I was relieved of the necessity of explaining them.

I am sorry if this sounds hard, but that is what living with your decisions means. Remember that when you went away you said, "I am of age and I don't need your permission to live with Joe"?

I said, "Judy, this is a big decision. Are you sure you can live with the consequences?"

You immediately answered, "What consequences? It's nobody's business."

For three months, living with your decision has simply meant living with a man with whom you think you are in love. It has meant having no mother to answer to and no one to tell you what to do or to act as your conscience.

Now, living with your decision means deciding what to do about family relationships

You are right of course when you say that your grandparents will be hurt. When two people celebrate a 50th anniversary as your grandparents are soon to do, it is because they long ago made an important decision. They committed themselves to one another. That gave love a chance to grow, to withstand the hard times and to survive for 50 years. You are right to think that people who have experienced this will have a hard time understanding what you call love.

You say that you love Joe and that you want to spend this part of your life with him even though neither of you is willing to commit yourself legally to the other for the rest of your lives. Judy, without commitment you do not have love. You have a relationship — and a fragile one at that. You know nothing of the real love experienced by two individuals who are willing to commit themselves to one another.

Without a commitment, there is no incentive to work at a relationship. In fact, the absence of commitment is contrary to the whole idea of developing a relationship. Without commitment there is no development, only questions: Is he the right one? Will I find someone I love more? Can I hold on to him? Do I dare make plans for next year? How long will it last?

When you commit yourself to someone, you enter the relationship knowing, "We are in this for better or for worse. It is to our advantage to work at it to make it the very best we can." On such decisions 50-year marriages are built.

Now my dear one, if you will think about these things, and if you will handle the anniversary party problem yourself, I promise I will consider the subject off limits in future letters. I love you.

Mom

Letter #2

A mother finds herself in the common position of having to watch a daughter suffer through a rocky romance. The mother has never approved of the relationship and has counseled seriously with the daughter on why it was not a good one. Still she loves her daughter and feels deeply for her during a painful period.

With a simple greeting card the mother conveys this message:

When you hurt,
I hurt.

Letter #3

A son has followed the narcotic trail to prison. While he had been aware of the possible results of his involvement, he had thought he could gamble and win. From prison he wrote his father that he had learned the hard way that his actions inevitably led to painful consequences. He could not, however, come to terms with his younger brothers having such a hard time in school because of what he had done. The father responds (in part):

> . . . It is interesting that you should say what you did about freedom — "Why can't we ever really be free to live our own life without having to worry about hurting those close to us?"

> I am sure you are referring to your brothers who are having such a bad time of it. Perhaps I can answer your question by sharing with you an ancient Jewish story. Several men went out in a rowboat. One man, lost in thought, began carving away with his knife on the floor of the boat. Suddenly one of the other men looked up and cried, "Stop that! You're cutting a hole in the bottom of the boat." And the fellow with the knife replied, "Leave me alone; I'm cutting this hole under my own seat."

> Sometimes when young people say, "I have the right to live the way I please," it translates, "I have the right to do what I please no matter who it hurts." This is a serious abuse of freedom, and anyone who lives like that will soon find himself very much alone . . .

Letter #4

This couple found that, although their son wanted to proceed with his life apart from the family, he could not accept the fact that they were rebuilding their own lives apart from him. He accused them of being angry with him, of rejecting him, and of cutting him off. The father tries to explain:

> Son,
>
> I am sorry you feel that we are angry with you. I'm afraid you really don't understand our feelings at all. What you did has not made us angry. It has not made us want to strike out at you. It broke our hearts and crushed our will to live. It brought your brother home from school because he could not carry on under the circumstances.
>
> When you love someone it is entirely possible to recognize his right to live his own life but still be crushed by what he is doing. For a time, all of us were incapable of functioning as a family at home, but we have come to realize we must change that.
>
> We never meant to convey that we were cutting you off. We will always love you, son, and something has gone out of our lives which no one can replace. Yet we must consider your brother at this point also. We have to pick up the pieces, pull together and rebuild our own lives. We hope you understand.
>
> Always,
> Dad

Letter #5

These Christian parents have watched their son slip farther and farther away from the family as he enters a lifestyle contrary to their sense of values. The immediate problem is that the son no longer keeps regular contact with his parents. The mother expresses their concern:

Dear son,

We are praying this will reach you. It has been so long since we have heard from you. Please, won't you try to keep in touch? No matter what your perception of our relationship is, we do love you very much. You might not feel this is true since we have refused to help you financially, but I'm sure you realize we simply cannot contribute to the lifestyle you have chosen. To just bum around, with all that word implies, to dabble on the fringes of the drug scene, and above all, to waste your excellent mind and many talents is, to us, unbelievable. It is hard for us to bear, impossible for us to support.

On the one hand, we want you to succeed with your rock group. On the other hand, we feel sure that you are not going to find happiness in that direction, even if you find success and fame.

I feel compelled to remind you that the Scripture says there is pleasure in sin for a season. If you are still reading—I'll add that, as a child of God, you will never find true peace or contentment while living in rebellion against Him. Besides, I hope you will think sometimes about how much God loves you. It is a comfort to us to know that God loves you even more than we do. His love is not dependent upon good behavior, and He knows all about your problems, your attitudes, why you have chosen your present course, and what it will take to turn you back to Him.

Now I promise, no more preaching. I'll just say we all miss you very, very much. Please do write us and let us know where you are and what you're doing. It is such a big world to lose a son in.

Lots of love,
Mom and Dad

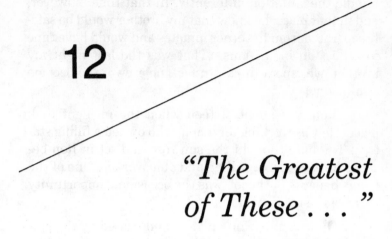

12

"The Greatest of These . . ."

To say that parental love takes many forms is to express nothing new. It has been said many times and in a variety of ways that a parent's love is not always verbalized but is communicated in other ways. For example, parents discipline because they love. That's why the lecture, "This hurts me worse than it does you," precedes the spanking. A child can't possibly believe the parent—the child has no comprehension of the amount of pain involved when a loving parent is forced to mete out such discipline.

My father is a no-nonsense person. He used firm disciplinary measures but he never appeared to me to be stern or unfeeling. Now that I look back, I can imagine that some of the discipline he handed out must have been very painful for him.

"Tough love"

Once he allowed my brother to spend the night in jail when he could easily have secured his release. Faced with the same decision today, my father would probably handle the situation differently. In that time, however, and in that place, he knew that my brother would be safely separated from the other inmates and would have time to reflect on his actions. (That was the last night my brother ever spent in jail. In fact, he grew up to become a minister.)

Ron was about sixteen when the incident took place. He was working for a man who owned a filling station. The man thought the sun rose and set in Ron because he was such a willing and able worker. One of the fringe benefits of the job was the occasional opportunity to drive the boss's pickup.

One evening Ron and a friend passed by the station and, seeing the truck, they decided to take a ride. The station was closed and the boss had gone home. The two boys climbed into the truck and drove off. (How can you ask permission if no one is around?)

Very shortly, someone notified the station owner that his pickup was gone, and called the police. Before you could say, "Juvenile delinquent," the boys were in the city jail.

My brother's boss was mortified. He refused to press charges. "Had I known it was Ron, it would have been okay. He can use that truck any time he wants to."

Yet the police refused to release my brother except into my father's custody. The owner called my dad and begged him to go get Ron. My mother dissolved into tears, and I watched the whole procedure realizing only that a crisis of great importance had confronted my parents.

In the midst of the confusion, my father made his decision. "Let him spend the night in jail," he said. "He had no business taking that truck without permission."

Only after I became a parent did I appreciate how hard it must have been for my father to do what he did.

In this book we have discussed some rather drastic decisions a parent must make, such as: "This is our home, Johnny, and you will not be allowed to destroy it." "It is your life, Johnny, and if you insist upon messing it up, we cannot stop you."

When spoken out of parental love, such decisions cause pain. It would not be painful to turn your back on Johnny if you did not love him. A great deal of pain is involved when you are forced to make heartbreaking decisions "for his good."

As the parents' love passes through the crucible of Johnny's rebellion, the parents must cling to the hope that someday Johnny will understand. Only in retrospect do children comprehend what their parents try to communicate through discipline: "I am doing this because I love you."

Experiencing parental love

To fully comprehend parental love, one must experience it from the giving end. My brother is the first-born in our family. I am next in line. When we were both in high school he coerced our parents into allowing him to join the Navy. When he left, my mother cried. All day. And all night. And the next day. And the next night. She cried so much that my father threatened to call the recruiting office to see if they ever inducted mothers.

Frankly, I couldn't understand her problem. At that stage of my life I thought that the Navy was a very convenient place for my brother to be. It was not until many years later when my husband and I took our firstborn off to college that I even began to sense the void my mother had felt when Ron left.

Parental love is something which children who experience it take for granted. The only children who are acutely conscious of something called parental love are those who are denied it.

My husband once counseled a young man who grew up in an affluent family from the upper social register in an Eastern state. By his own definition, this young man lived a typical poor-little-rich-boy existence. As a child he was conscious that he had everything except his parents' time and the love it represented.

I, on the other hand, grew up taking for granted that my parents loved me. I gave it little thought because I assumed everyone had that kind of family. When I went to college I began to see that there were many young people whose home situations were vastly different. Only then did I consciously verbalize what I had always accepted: "My parents love me."

Remembering how I took my own parents for granted helped me survive some of those experiences I faced as a mother of teens. As our girls were entering their teenage years I took pen in hand one day and with tongue in cheek penned these words:

As a mother of girls who have reached their teen years, I sometimes find myself examining their actions and words for the barest hint that I am loved, or at least needed, but teenagers express such things only in books. Parents of teenagers are seldom loved and almost never appreciated. At best, they are tolerated, and our only encouragement may come in the signs that our teens are mostly more tolerant than their peers.

I wrote it in a rather tolerant mood of my own, but as time went on it became more difficult to be philosophical about teenage attitudes toward parents. The memory of my own attitude toward my parents sustained me many times. As a teenager I went through all the various stages—the critical, the impudent, and the condescending. With each phase I am sure I must have made it painfully clear that I considered my parents totally inadequate for their job. I doubted many things about them during those phases of the teenage uglies, but somehow it never occurred to me to doubt their love.

If parents did not love, they would not cry. Parental heartache is vividly described by one father who wrote of seeing his son destroy himself on heroin before he was old enough to vote. Recalling one scene with a psychiatrist, the father stated that the doctor turned to the mother and demanded, "Why are you crying? That kind of emotional reaction is not going to help." And the father commented on this scene, "Her firstborn shooting himself full of heroin, and the doctor asks, 'Why are you crying?'!"

There is but one answer for those who would stem the flow of parental tears altogether: Do away with parenthood.

Earlier in this book I referred to a young woman who opted for non-parenthood because of the risk involved. She asked herself, "Am I emotionally equipped to face the risk of losing a child through teenage rebellion?" Another young woman of my acquaintance asked herself the question, "Could I have a child and not abuse him?" (She had been an abused child.) In each case these women came up with the same answer. The only way to avoid the risk is to avoid parenthood altogether.

The risk of loving

Certainly there is an unknown quantity involved in giving life to a child. There is no clause on the birth certificate warning the parents, "This model will self-destruct in fifteen years or less. To avoid injury to parent, do not attach too closely." Parental love is a risk. In fact, any kind of love is a risk.

Love is a risk because it involves a relationship. There are many things in life which we may prefer to do with another person but which we can do just as well alone. We can live alone, eat alone, work alone, travel alone—none of these demands a relationship—but we cannot love alone. If we love, there is at least one other person involved. Love demands a relationship.

With every relationship there is the potential for sorrow as well as for joy. This is more evident in a parent-child relationship because it is more permanent. Other relationships are often dropped when something goes wrong.

Yesterday I read the case history of a woman who terminated a friendship with another woman because she felt it was not a good relationship. They had widely differing personal goals which impeded the natural progress of the friendship. So it was set aside. Discontinued. End of relationship. End of problem.

With a parent-child relationship it cannot be so. You cannot set aside this relationship simply because the tears have begun to outweigh the laughter. When it becomes obvious that parent and child have widely different personal goals and the result is a deteriorating relationship, the parent does not simply quit loving the child and end the relationship. Because we continue to love, we must sometimes continue to cry.

Preserving parental love

If you can define a gift as something which costs the giver, then you can define parental love accurately as a gift. I have come to see that the love of my parents is the most valuable gift they ever gave to me.

When we own something of value, it is normal to take precautions to preserve it. We furnished our home primarily with things which were once best described as "family attic." With the passing of time, we have reclassified some of the castoffs as American antique.

One of our favorite pieces is an oak secretary complete with a round glass door. It once belonged to my mother-in-law. She protected the glass door from a lot of little hands over the years and preserved it intact. At the time she decided she had no more use for it, it was worth, at most, about $65. Today it is worth a dozen times that. We have continued to preserve the cabinet by protecting the glass from misplaced furniture, careless movers and more uncontrolled little hands. Because we did not allow our children to destroy it, one day we expect to pass it on to one of them.

Parental love is a thing of great value. Great pain should be taken to preserve it. You may lose the battle to preserve Johnny's morals. You may stand helplessly by as he ruins his health. Your hands may be tied as he jeopardizes his future. You may even lose his love for you — but you must not lose your love for him.

Parents do not normally think in terms of preserving their love for their children. Instead, they spend a lot of time and emotional energy trying to preserve Johnny's love for them. They become frustrated, disillusioned and even bitter because it is a losing battle. Of far more importance is the preservation of their love for their child.

If I could give just one word of advice to parents faced with the heartbreak of rebellion, it would be this: Do not allow your child to so abuse your love that he destroys it. If he destroys your love for him, you will both have lost something of inestimable value.

When our middle daughter was living at home just before her marriage, she had the delightful habit of leaving quotations, which she had typed on little pieces of paper, on my mirror or my bulletin board. One such quotation (source unknown) reads

We are, most of us, very lonely in this world; you who have any who love you, cling to them and thank God.

Parents of estranged children must hope for the future—that one day Johnny will realize the truth of this quotation. When that day comes, he still needs to be able to number his parents among those who love him.

Your can preserve your love for Johnny if you take charge of your life, your home, your future. These are not selfish measures. The parent who has the courage to take whatever action necessary to control these things will preserve something else that is precious as well. Finding life after Johnny will, in the end, allow the parents to go on loving Johnny.

The gift of love

One particular biblical passage has been memorized again and again because of its description of love. Known as the "Love Chapter," 1 Corinthians 13 also has been the basis of countless paraphrases. I offer here yet one more, my personal version of parental love based on 1 Corinthians 13.

A Mother's Paraphrase of 1 Corinthians 13

If I speak in the vernacular of my teens
and understand the language of their peers,
but do not give them love,
I am just like so much noise
falling on their ears.

If I could tell my children
exactly what their future holds,
if I knew everything ahead of them,
and if I believed that someday
each one of them would make it,
but did not give them love,
I am nothing.

If I give them everything they want,
if I sacrifice all I have—even my life—for them,
and give not love,
they gain nothing.

Parental love is patient
even with erring offspring.
It is kind to the daughter who is hurting.
It never says, "I told you so."
Parental love is not rude to the impudent son
nor easily angered by his ways.
Parental love does not delight
in father's dire predictions
which have come to pass,
but rejoices at the slightest positive sign
in the child who strays.
Parental love protects the toddler,
firmly guides the adolescent,
hopes for those who falter
and perseveres year after year.

Parental love should never fail.
Our plans for the future may fail.
Our advice may be stilled.

Our knowledge may fall short.
For we do not know everything
and we cannot control everyone—
but we can love.

When I was a young mother,
I was a visionary.
I had all the answers and knew all the formulas
for successful child-rearing.
But when my children were grown
I put those immature ideas behind me.
Now I have no answers.
I know so little
and my understanding is so limited.
Only in Heaven can I know the rest.
There my understanding shall be complete,
my joy will be full
and my tears will be wiped away.

Three things I have now—
faith
that my children will remember their training,
hope
that this will influence their future,
and love
that continues no matter what.

And the greatest of these is love.

© 1979, by Joy P. Gage, Yuma, Arizona

Love is a risk, and love costs the giver something—but love is the greatest gift a parent can give.

Postscript . . .

For my daughters —

*I have sometimes not understood you
and I have often disagreed with you
but I have always loved you.*

Reference Notes

Chapter 1. When Parents Cry

1. Adapted from the *Yuma Daily Sun*, May 16, 1979.

Chapter 4. Politics, Peers and Parental Pressures

1. Will Durant, *Caesar and Christ* (New York: Simon and Schuster, 1944), p. 531.

2. "What's Happening to the American Family?" *Better Homes and Gardens* (May 1973), p. 2.

Chapter 5. Perpetuating Parental Values in the Home

1. "Healthy Criticism: Crossing the Age Barrier and Communicating With Your Children." *Today's Health* (August, 1973), p. 72.

Chapter 7. Eight Do's and Don'ts for the Post-Crisis Period

1. "How to Survive Your Adolescent," *Reader's Digest* (March, 1973, an interview with Dr. Martin Symonds, by Joan Rattner Heilman), p. 106.

Chapter 9. Can We Begin Again, Lord?

1. Ruth Bell Graham, *Sitting By My Laughing Fire* (Waco, TX: Word Books, 1977), p. 47. Used by permission.

2. © 1959 by Manna Music, Inc., 2111 Kenmere Ave, Burbank, CA 91504. International copyright secured. All rights reserved. Used by permission.

Chapter 10. We Still Have Each Other

1. Jim Conway, *Men in Mid-Life Crisis* (Elgin, IL: David C. Cook, 1978), p. 184.

2. Conway, p. 180.

3. Kathryn Haveisen, "Death of a Fairy Tale," *Home Life* (September 1978), p. 45.

Chapter 12. "The Greatest of These . . ."

1. "What Did I Do Wrong?" *Today's Health* (August 1973), p. 41.

153

APPENDIX

Have You Made the Wonderful Discovery of the Spirit-Filled Life?

You may obtain copies of the Campus Crusade for Christ booklet from which this adaptation is taken at Christian bookstores or from the publisher.

EVERY DAY CAN BE AN EXCITING ADVENTURE FOR THE CHRISTIAN who knows the reality of being filled with the Holy Spirit and who lives constantly, moment by moment, under His gracious direction.

The Bible tells us that there are three kinds of people:

1. NATURAL MAN

(One who has not received Christ)

"But a natural man does not accept the things of the Spirit of God; for they are foolishness to him, and he cannot understand them, because they are spiritually appraised" (1 Corinthians 2:14).

SELF-DIRECTED LIFE

S - Ego or finite self is on the throne
† - Christ is outside the life
● - Interests are directed by self, often resulting in discord and frustration

2. SPIRITUAL MAN

(One who is directed and empowered by the Holy Spirit)

"But he who is spiritual appraises all things . . ." (1 Corinthians 2:15).

CHRIST-DIRECTED LIFE

† - Christ is in the life and on the throne
S - Self is yielding to Christ
● - Interests are directed by Christ, resulting in harmony with God's plan

3. CARNAL MAN

(One who has received Christ, but who lives in defeat because he trusts in his own efforts to live the Christian life)

"And I, brethren, could not speak to you as to spiritual men, but as to carnal men, as to babes in Christ. I gave you milk to drink, not solid food; for you were not yet able to receive it. Indeed, even now you are not yet able, for you are still carnal. For since there is jealousy and strife among you, are you not fleshly, and are you not walking like mere men?" (1 Corinthians 3:1-3).

SELF-DIRECTED LIFE

S - Self is on the throne
† - Christ dethroned and not allowed to direct the life
● - Interests are directed by self, often resulting in discord and frustration

1 GOD HAS PROVIDED FOR US AN ABUNDANT AND FRUITFUL CHRISTIAN LIFE.

Jesus said, "I came that they might have life, and might have it abundantly" (John 10:10).

"I am the vine, you are the branches; he who abides in Me, and I in him, he bears much fruit; for apart from Me you can do nothing" (John 15:5).

"But the fruit of the Spirit is love, joy, peace, patience, kindness, goodness, faithfulness, gentleness, self-control; against such things there is no law" (Galatians 5:22,23).

"But you shall receive power when the Holy Spirit has come upon you; and you shall be My witnesses both in Jerusalem, and in all Judea and Samaria, and even to the remotest part of the earth" (Acts 1:8).

THE SPIRITUAL MAN – Some personal traits which result from trusting God:

Christ-centered
Empowered by the Holy Spirit
Introduces others to Christ
Effective prayer life
Understands God's Word
Trusts God
Obeys God
Love
Joy
Peace
Patience
Kindness
Faithfulness
Goodness

The degree to which these traits are manifested in the life depends upon the extent to which the Christian trusts the Lord with every detail of his life, and upon his maturity in Christ. One who is only beginning to understand the ministry of the Holy Spirit should not be discouraged if he is not as fruitful as more mature Christians who have known and experienced this truth for a longer period.

Why is it that most Christians are not experiencing the abundant life?

2 CARNAL CHRISTIANS CANNOT EXPERIENCE THE ABUNDANT AND FRUITFUL CHRISTIAN LIFE.

The carnal man trusts in his own efforts to live the Christian life:

A. He is either uninformed about, or has forgotten, God's love, forgiveness and power (Romans 5:8-10; Hebrews 10:1-25; 1 John 1; 2:1-3; 2 Peter 1:9; Acts 1:8).

B. He has an up-and-down spiritual experience.

C. He cannot understand himself – he wants to do what is right, but cannot.

D. He fails to draw upon the power of the Holy Spirit to live the Christian life (1 Corinthians 3:1-3; Romans 7:15-24; 8:7; Galatians 5:16-18).

THE CARNAL MAN – Some or all of the following traits may characterize the Christian who does not fully trust God:

Ignorance of his spiritual heritage
Unbelief
Disobedience
Loss of love for God and for others
Poor prayer life
No desire for Bible study
Legalistic attitude
Impure thoughts
Jealousy
Guilt
Worry
Discouragement
Critical spirit
Frustration
Aimlessness

(The individual who professes to be a Christian but who continues to practice sin should realize that he may not be a Christian at all, according to 1 John 2:3; 3:6,9; Ephesians 5:5.)

The third truth gives us the only solution to this problem . . .

3 JESUS PROMISED THE ABUNDANT AND FRUITFUL LIFE AS THE RESULT OF BEING FILLED (DIRECTED AND EMPOWERED) BY THE HOLY SPIRIT.

The Spirit-filled life is the Christ-directed life by which Christ lives His life in and through us in the power of the Holy Spirit (John 15).

A. One becomes a Christian through the ministry of the Holy Spirit, according to John 3:1-8. From the moment of spiritual birth, the Christian is indwelt by the Holy Spirit at all times (John 1:12; Colossians 2:9,10; John 14:16,17).

Though all Christians are indwelt by the Holy Spirit, not all Christians are filled (directed and empowered) by the Holy Spirit on an ongoing basis.

B. The Holy Spirit is the source of the overflowing life (John 7:37-39).

C. The Holy Spirit came to glorify Christ (John 16:1-15). When one is filled with the Holy Spirit, he is a true disciple of Christ.

D. In His last command before His ascension, Christ promised the power of the Holy Spirit to enable us to be witnesses for Him (Acts 1:1-9).

How, then, can one be filled with the Holy Spirit?

4 WE ARE FILLED (DIRECTED AND EMPOWERED) BY THE HOLY SPIRIT BY FAITH; THEN WE CAN EXPERIENCE THE ABUNDANT AND FRUITFUL LIFE WHICH CHRIST PROMISED TO EACH CHRISTIAN.

You can appropriate the filling of the Holy Spirit **right now** if you:

A. Sincerely desire to be directed and empowered by the Holy Spirit (Matthew 5:6; John 7:37-39).

B. Confess your sins. By **faith** thank God that He **has** forgiven all of your sins — past, present and future — because Christ died for you (Colossians 2:13-15; 1 John 1; 2:1-3; Hebrews 10:1-17).

C. Present every area of your life to God (Romans 12:1,2).

D. By **faith** claim the fullness of the Holy Spirit, according to:

1. HIS COMMAND — Be filled with the Spirit. "And do not get drunk with wine, for that is dissipation, but be filled with the Spirit" (Ephesians 5:18).

2. HIS PROMISE — He will always answer when we pray according to His will. "And this is the confidence which we have before Him, that, if we ask anything according to His will, He hears us. And if we know that He hears us in whatever we ask, we know that we have the requests which we have asked from Him" (1 John 5:14,15).

Faith can be expressed through prayer . . .

How to Pray in Faith to Be Filled With the Holy Spirit

We are filled with the Holy Spirit by **faith** alone. However, true prayer is one way of expressing your faith. The following is a suggested prayer:

> "Dear Father, I need You. I acknowledge that I have been directing my own life and that, as a result, I have sinned against You. I thank You that You have forgiven my sins through Christ's death on the cross for me. I now invite Christ to again take His place on the throne of my life. Fill me with the Holy Spirit as You **commanded** me to be filled, and as You **promised** in Your Word that You would do if I asked in faith. I pray this in the name of Jesus. As an expression of my faith, I now thank You for directing my life and for filling me with the Holy Spirit."

Does this prayer express the desire of your heart? If so, bow in prayer and trust God to fill you with the Holy Spirit **right now.**

How to Know That You Are Filled (Directed and Empowered) by the Holy Spirit

Did you ask God to fill you with the Holy Spirit? Do you know that you are now filled with the Holy Spirit? On what authority? (On the trustworthiness of God Himself and His Word: Hebrews 11:6; Romans 14:22,23.)

Do not depend upon feelings. The promise of God's Word, not our feelings, is our authority. The Christian lives by faith (trust) in the trustworthiness of God Himself and His Word.

This train diagram illustrates the relationship between **fact** (God and His Word), **faith** (our trust in God and His Word), and **feeling** (the result of our faith and obedience) (John 14:21).

The train will run with or without the caboose. However, it would be futile to attempt to pull the train by the caboose. In the same way, we, as Christians, do not depend upon feelings or emotions, but we place our faith (trust) in the trustworthiness of God and the promises of His Word.

How to Walk in the Spirit

Faith (trust in God and in His promises) is the only means by which a Christian can live the Spirit-directed life. As you continue to trust Christ moment by moment:

A. Your life will demonstrate more and more of the fruit of the Spirit (Galatians 5:22,23) and will be more and more conformed to the image of Christ (Romans 12:2; 2 Corinthians 3:18).

B. Your prayer life and study of God's Word will become more meaningful.

C. You will experience His power in witnessing (Acts 1:8).

D. You will be prepared for spiritual conflict against the world (1 John 2:15-17); against the flesh (Galatians 5:16,17); and against Satan (1 Peter 5:7-9; Ephesians 6:10-13).

E. You will experience His power to resist temptation and sin (1 Corinthians 10:13; Philippians 4:13; Ephesians 1:19-23; 6:10; 2 Timothy 1:7; Romans 6:1-16).

Spiritual Breathing

By faith you can continue to experience God's love and forgiveness.

If you become aware of an area of your life (an attitude or an action) that is displeasing to the Lord, even though you are walking with Him and sincerely desiring to serve Him, simply thank God that He has forgiven your sins — past, present and future — on the basis of Christ's death on the cross. Claim His love and forgiveness by faith and continue to have fellowship with Him.

If you retake the throne of your life through sin — a definite act of disobedience — breathe spiritually.

Spiritual Breathing (exhaling the impure and inhaling the pure) is an exercise in faith and enables you to continue to experience God's love and forgiveness.

1. **Exhale** — confess your sin — agree with God concerning your sin and thank Him for His forgiveness of it, according to 1 John 1:9 and Hebrews 10:1-25. Confession involves repentance — a change in attitude and action.

2. **Inhale** — surrender the control of your life to Christ, and appropriate (receive) the fullness of the Holy Spirit by faith. Trust that He now directs and empowers you, according to the **command** of Ephesians 5:18 and the **promise** of 1 John 5:14,15.

* * * * *

> *To help you make the most of your relationship with God, you may wish to obtain THE SECRET: HOW TO LIVE WITH PURPOSE AND POWER by Bill Bright.*
> *This book is available in Christian bookstores everywhere, or you may call 1-800-950-4HLP and order directly from the publisher.*

(© Campus Crusade for Christ, Inc. 1966. All rights reserved.)

*One topic strikes fear in the heart
of every parent...*

Talking With Your Kids About Love, Sex and Dating

Barry and Carol St. Clair

For many, the fear of "the talk" — a nervous, one-time chat with their children about sex — becomes overwhelming. Let Barry and Carol St. Clair show you how you can resolve those fears and how to address the underlying issues of sexuality through effective, ongoing communication with your children.

Talking With Your Kids offers specific outlines for conversations about:

- What happens when their bodies change
- How far is too far
- How to make dating decisions
- How to handle sexual pressure
- And more!

More than just helping you survive "the talk," Barry and Carol give you the practical guidance to build an atmosphere of love, trust and interaction with your kids on these vital topics.

At Christian bookstores everywhere.

Or call

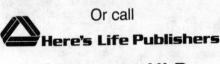 **Here's Life Publishers**

1-800-950-4HLP

Visa and Mastercard accepted.

*Straight Talk to Teens
From Barry St. Clair and Bill Jones*

DATING, LOVE & SEX

Making the Right Decisions for a Great Relationship
(Josh McDowell, Series Editor)

The bestselling three-book gift set that parents and youth workers nationwide are giving to their teens. Popular youth speakers Barry St. Clair and Bill Jones offer sound advice and straight answers to the questions teens are asking.

The set includes **Dating: Picking (and Being) a Winner**, **Sex: Desiring the Best**, and **Love: Making It Last**, together in an attractive slipcover. It's an ideal gift that will help your teen understand why God's ways make sense.

Each book is also available individually.

At Christian bookstores everywhere.

Or call

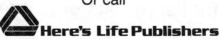

Here's Life Publishers

1-800-950-4HLP

Visa and Mastercard accepted.

Pulling Weeds, Planting Seeds

Growing Character in Your Life and Family

Dennis Rainey

Living the Christian life is like growing a garden: It requires steady, careful cultivation. As a father of six, Dennis Rainey recognizes that excellence in personal and family life doesn't happen naturally. Weeds must be pulled and seeds must be planted so that the fruit of the Spirit can thrive.

Writing with personal transparency, Dennis Rainey inspires you to "pull weeds" and "plant seeds" in your own life and in the lives of your family members. This no-holds-barred appeal for commitment to personal and family growth is recommended for individual study, husband/wife interaction and group discussion.

> **"Pulling Weeds, Planting Seeds** is a thought-provoking blend of God-given truths, memorable nostalgia, and homemade happiness . . . A more fruitful harvest awaits all who will take the time to read and heed these pages."
>
> **Cynthia Swindoll**
> Executive Vice President
> Insight for Living

At Christian bookstores everywhere.

Or call

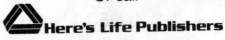
Here's Life Publishers

1-800-950-4HLP

Visa and Mastercard accepted.